Reflections on Time

From the Seasons of My Life

Philip Stover

Printed in the United States of America

First Printing, 2016

ISBN 978-0-9904554-3-1

Rio Vista Press
713 W Spruce St PMB 127
Deming, NM 88030

All photographs are the property of the author, are used with
permission, or are in the public domain. A few names have been
changed or left out.

Cover Design by Philip Stover

Other Books by Philip Stover:

*Religion and Revolution in Mexico's North: Even Unto Death . . .
Tengamos Fe*. It is available on Amazon and at your local bookstore.
(eBook and paperback)

Mata Ortiz Pottery: A Buyer's Guide, a practical guide for the
enthusiast and collector of Mata Ortiz pottery. (eBook and
paperback)

www.riovistapress.com

Table of Contents

This little book is dedicated to Brandon, Tyler, Dick, Brad, Russell, and all the other guys and gals of the first and second watch convergence gatherings. I learned so much from each of you. The fellowship was amazing. I even won a Girard Perregaux Sea Hawk!

I dedicate these stories to all the guys and gals on Timezone.com who have helped me, answered my innumerable questions, and showed me their horological knowhow! Thanks to each of you.

Lastly, I dedicate this to all the members of the National Association of Watch and Clock Collectors. You also have taught me much. Your collective expertise is amazing! Thank you!

These stories are for all of you!

It seems they had always been and would always be, friends. Time could change much, but not that. Winnie the Pooh

One life; a little gleam of Time between two Eternities . . . Thomas Carlyle

May God grant me the grace, wisdom, and judgment to use my time well.

May I not be burdened by the need to achieve more things, but by the desire to achieve better things.

May I have the passion not to climb the ladder for myself, but to hold the ladder for others.

May I desire not to create taller buildings, but stronger foundations.

From *Reflections on Time* by Philip Stover

Preface

My interests in clocks began around 1968. For some reason unremembered, one day I went into an old guy's antique shop in Siloam Springs, Arkansas where I was a college sophomore. I saw a very cool old mantle clock. It looked as old as the gray bearded proprietor of the shop. Well, maybe not that old. . . . Why I bought it I will never know. How I had the money to buy it I will never know. Anyway, I did. I took it back to my dorm room. I shined it up and it became my prize possession (next to my twelve string guitar). I sold my guitar to buy an engagement ring for my wife-to-be, but I kept that clock for many years. It went with us through lots of graduate schools, jobs, and assorted journeys in life. I don't know where it is now. I hope it found a happy home.

These stories started in 2002. I had become fascinated by watches, especially those with any kind of map on the dial. EBay and a host of other websites fed my appetite for map dial watches.

The Author's First Map Dial Watch

I became the guru of map dial watches, most of which I could not afford but all of which I could drool over. I began posting on watch collecting forums, bragging about my latest acquisition and lamenting the one I had missed or couldn't find. I began going to every NAWCC (National Association of Watch and Clock Collectors) convention I could find. I was doing school district consulting at that time so I always checked the local area where I was working for any watch shows. Watch shows are kind of like Comic-Con for old white guys. To belong you must have a beard, an old khaki vest, and some kind of goofy hat. I didn't have a beard, bought an old L. L. Bean vest, and liked Indiana Jones-style fedoras, so I soon sort of belonged. I was hooked. I soon became known as the map dial watch guy and sellers would look for me at the shows. How many map dial watches are there? I don't know, but I probably have photos of at least 200 different ones on my computer to this day.

Then I branched out into pocket watches. Not map dial pocket watches, but pocket watches that are known at the watch shows as private label pocket watches. Lots of pocket watch companies made watches for jewelry, clothing, or department stores. They were private labelled with the name and location of the store on the dial. I was hooked when I began to look for one private label watch from each state. I was determined to be one of only two people I knew on the planet who had a private label watch from each state. EBay became my hunting ground. Watch shows now knew me as the map dial – private label guy. Dear reader, even if you cared, do you have any idea how hard it is to find a private label pocket watch from North Dakota, Wyoming, or Alaska? As a young man I was determined to visit all fifty states. I accomplished that when I made a mad fun trip to North and South Dakota one weekend when working in the Chicago area. Now, a middle age nut job, I was determined to have a private label watch from each state! I kept an Excel spreadsheet of my conquests. I never made it!

Waltham North Dakota Private Label Pocket Watch

According to my old Excel spreadsheet I got to thirty-two states when I got into an economic predicament and had to sell my private label pocket watches and most of my map dial watches. For a month or so I flooded the market with the same! Now as I write this, some sixteen years later, I am overcome with a strange urge to start over again. Now where would I find a Chihuahua private label pocket watch? Get thee behind me Comic-Con-watch-show-khaki-vest-wearing-man!

Just a bit more personal history to help you understand how these stories came to be. I grew up the son of a preacher-man. I majored in history and Bible in college and went to several seminaries and graduate schools in religious studies. I then taught college where I specialized in two academic areas, both of which will bore the reader almost as much as private label pocket watches! My specialties were the integration of psychology and theology, and the teaching of homiletics. Before you grab for your dictionary (maybe Kindle defines homiletics?) let me define it for you; homiletics is the study of preaching – verbal communication from the pulpit. An individual sermon is a homily As a boy it was the boring part of Sunday, listening to my father (or any other preacher for that matter) before we went home to Sunday dinner, always the culinary highlight of the week. Sunday was the only day we had dinner; every other day we had lunch or supper. Whatever happened to Sunday dinners? I think they have gone the way of private label pocket watches! Then I preached my first sermon at age 16 and I was hooked. I really enjoyed public speaking, but especially preaching. I pastored, where preaching is a weekly activity and enjoyed teaching preaching (I am a poet at heart).

At some point early in 2002 I decided, just for fun I would write some non-sectarian sermons (homilies) about time. They were designed to amuse and hopefully, inspire my watch collecting friends. I called them horological homilies and produced one a week for about a year. Now just in case Sunday morning sermons bored you as a child too, these were more like short stories than sermons. Some of them were lost in computer transitions, but I managed to keep about 40 Word files, each populated with a homily. My wife continually and regularly encouraged me to put them together in a little book. Life got in the way. The role of a senior administrator in large public school districts leaves one little time for khaki vests. I think, however I was the resident Will Rogers (humorist), Ambrose Bierce (satirist), and Phil Stover (punista extraordinaire) for a number of school boards who were just as bored with their meetings as was everyone else in attendance.

Now I am retired from all of that. So I got out my old external hard drive, found the homilies and this little book is the result. I thought several times about updating the stories because some of them are fourteen years old. I finally decided against it. If they have kernels of truth in them, then that truth is as real today as it was years ago. I truly hope you enjoy the stories and the lessons they hope to teach. Some are very short, while others go on for a while. Read them one at a time or in an hour or two you can probably read them all. They are not overly theological, but there are regular mentions of God. The purpose is not to tell you how to view God in your own life. That is a very personal decision. I share some of myself in these stories making them a bit biographical. I hope none of that offends you, the reader. These stories are from the seasons of my life. As such, they are often about change, or the desire for change. Most of all I hope they make you smile and as the snow, trees, and sun from the cover photo (our back yard) help you reflect on your own life.

Oh, and by the way, if you ever find a South Dakota private label pocket watch or a watch with a map of Mexico on it, let me know! I don't think I could resist them! Now where is that old vest?

Using Time Well

It is approximately 350 miles from the Sarasota/Bradenton area to Jackson County, Florida. My company has a contract with the Jackson County School District. Jackson County is in Florida's panhandle, the most beautiful (in my opinion), and least visited part of our state. I make the trip at least once a month. On a good day, the trip takes me six hours each way. It costs approximately $91.00 roundtrip (four tanks of gas and two stops at the Brooksville Wendy's for a single hamburger, small chili, Dr. Pepper and a small Frosty). I am a Wendy's man. My wife isn't too jealous. I always come home to her.

On Thursday, October 12, 1865, Dr. Charles Hentz left his home in Quincy, Florida for a visit to some friends in the Sarasota/Bradenton area. Dr. Hentz was a very prominent Jackson/Gadsden County physician. He had never been to the Tampa Bay area. Hentz set out in the company of two friends and his former slave (now his paid servant and friend). Fortunately for us, Dr. Hentz was a prolific writer. He has left us a 620 page autobiography and diary. It is probably our best single window into life on the frontier of Florida in the mid-nineteenth century.

They reached Tampa on Wednesday, October 25. Averaging a steady 25 miles a day, it took them approximately two weeks to make the one-way trip. They followed the same basic route that I travel once a month. They faced hunger, storms, and hostile strangers (well, maybe the trips aren't that dissimilar!). They lost their frying pan. This was a disaster as it kept them from easily cooking the squirrels they shot on the way.

And yes they also stopped at Brooksville, according to the map in his journal very close to the exact site of my Wendy's. Surrounded there by a pack of wolves, they shuddered through the night, keeping their fire brightly burning. Rivers, creeks, and streams that I barely notice were major obstacles for them.

We think the economy is bad now, yet 1865 was post-war Florida and things were really tight. This is witnessed by a sign, noticed by Dr. Hentz that was nailed to a tree on the banks of the Suwannee River. Writing that, "The schoolmaster is evidently out down here," Dr. Hentz couldn't resist recording the sign verbatim in his diary: *"enny pursan Can Cros the river at new troy at enny time as Chep as enny fary on the river for the manney, corn or mele or enny thing that I can yuse. Tomes walker his fary"*

Dr. Hentz and friends enjoyed their sojourn in the Sarasota/Bradenton area (who wouldn't?). They journeyed back to Quincy, gratefully arriving home in mid-November. Hentz kept meticulous financial records on the trip. The total round trip, including their stay in Bradenton, cost them $91.96. Does that sound familiar? Maybe times haven't changed all that much!

Why do I tell you this tale of an obscure vacation trip in the mid-nineteenth century? Because, when I read it, I was really impressed with how much more time we have available to us today. Their difficult two-week trip takes me a delightful six hours.

Then I was hit with a twinge of guilt (remember I am Mennonite, so guilt comes easily!). I questioned myself on whether, with all my modern advantages, I have accomplished anywhere near as much as my friend, Dr. Hentz. He treated many patients (almost always after a long journey to their homes), wrote a 600 page book (with quill and ink while I am sitting here drinking tea and using my laptop), wrote over 100 treatises on "modern medicine," was a Grand Master of his Masonic Lodge, lay-chair of his Methodist church, and recorded many wonderful day-long picnics with his family and friends. It seems that every other page of his diary has him enjoying a drink of lemonade on his veranda with some friend or family member. How did he do it all?

This is not a treatise on how we should do more or be busier. The good Lord knows I couldn't stand that. It is, instead, the mere posing of a question. With all the blessings of our modern day conveniences how is it that we so often wish for more time to accomplish this or that? Yet, how many of us reflect on the day's events in diaries, enjoy lemonade, or regularly take day-long picnics with our families?

I enjoy Wendy's. I have never encountered a wolf. I write with my laptop with cursor and pixels, not with quill and paper. I am growing a company not guiding a community. I drive my Ford above the rivers; I don't cross the rivers at the ford (clever, huh?).

I have so much more time; yet I seem to need so much more time. I use my chronograph to determine elapsed time and then have a fit at how much time has elapsed.

May God grant me the grace, wisdom, and judgment to use my time well. May I not be burdened by the need to achieve more things, but by the desire to achieve better things. May I have the passion not to climb the ladder for myself, but to hold the ladder for others. May I desire not to create taller buildings, but stronger foundations.

May God help me use my time well.

Amen and Amen

Things and People are not Always as They Seem!

I think I am getting disillusioned about watches....

It seems like we are hearing more and more about how things are not always as they appear to be in the world of watch advertising. For example:

- "Water resistant" - Then the directions tell me not to wear it in the shower!
- "Manufacturer" - Perhaps at best means "assembler"
- "Swiss-Made" - Perhaps at best means "Some Asian parts - Swiss assembled"
- "German-Made" - See "Swiss-Made"
- "Jewels" - Synthetic rubies . . . not jewels at all
- "Alligator Grain" - Calf leather stamped to look like the denizens of Florida
- "Sapphlex Crystal" - Who knows what that means????
- "Rare" - I have to sell this puppy today
- "LNIB" (Like New in Box) - I just bought this box and put my year old watch in it to sell
- "Vintage" – I have to sell this old beat up watch (the equivalent of "cozy" in describing a house for sale)
- "Gray Market" – Any watch that is being sold at a better discount than the dealer in front of me will offer

And so on . . . .

But before I get too discouraged about watch hype not always being an accurate reflection of reality, I might want to look at myself; what my words and my actions are saying:

- "I'll have it for you in a minute" - I haven't started on it yet
- "I'll be home in just a few minutes" - At least half an hour
- "You look nice" - I really wish you would wear something else
- "I have lots of experience" - I am over 50
- "The check is in the mail" - I get paid tomorrow and I will mail it out then
- "You can count on me" - I have never done this before and I sure hope I don't screw up
- "You didn't tell me to stop and bring home bread" - I forgot to get the bread
- "I would never do that" - I haven't done it yet . . . or . . . I haven't got caught doing it yet
- "What, this watch? I've had it forever" - UPS delivered it just before my wife got home. She just noticed it

Let's all remember to look to ourselves before we are critical of others. Let us not have 20-20 vision when scrutinizing others and be blinded when seeing ourselves. Carl Rogers, the great therapist of the 1950's and 1960's said that we all have an ideal self (how we see ourselves) and a real self (how we really are). The bigger the gap between the two, the more stress we cause ourselves and those around us. May we all have the courage, strength, and wisdom to get our ideal self and our real self as closely aligned as possible.

One of the authors I enjoy the most is Father John Powell, a Jesuit priest. The following is one of my favorite quotes from his writings:

"Blessed is he who has learned to laugh at himself for he shall never cease to be entertained." ***Amen and Amen***

A Holiday Horological Homily

Santa frowned a big frown. That was quite hard for him to do. His face muscles were not used to frowns. They were much more comfortable making those big jelly belly laughs. Santa frowned because he had a Christmas wish list that he just could not satisfy. Now, Santa could fill just about anybody's special wish list, but not this one, not this time. Santa paused. Santa sighed. "Some things are just beyond my capabilities," he thought to himself.

Santa had just received the Christmas wish list from Phil in sunny Florida. Actually Santa loved the Florida part of his trip. He always enjoyed flying low over the azure gulf. He liked the fact that the chimneys were not very hot. In fact, there were not many fireplaces in Florida period.

Rudolf, on the other hand wasn't too thrilled with the Florida leg of the trip. Reindeer, palm trees, and humidity just didn't mix in his mind! He couldn't wait to get to Finland to see all his cousins, aunts, and uncles. Lapland was Rudolf's favorite part of the annual global excursion. But that is another story.

Phil had been a good boy (well, sort of) all year (well, most of it). Santa read Phil's list with a mixture of emotions:

Dear Santa:

I want more time this year to:

1. Spend with those I love

2. Help bring about peace on earth (or just within my own home would be fine)

3. Be kind and less mean

4. Be more vulnerable with less hiding behind masks

5. Be more caring with less gossip

6. Learn more faith with less religiosity

7. Pursue more being with less doing

8. Be sincere and pursue less stuff (yes even fewer watches)

9. Be more understanding and less judgmental

10. Focus more on others and less on myself

Santa was at a loss. Ten requests and he couldn't meet even one of them! He had lots of watches, clocks, sundials, and the like, but he had no time in his bag. He couldn't give even one person even one more second of time.

Santa even felt a twinge of guilt. His bag was full of toy guns, tanks, and soldiers. He knew that real soldiers are real people. He knew that wars hurt. He hoped that his simple toys wouldn't help people to forget that. His bag was full of toys but a little short on time. He wondered aloud to himself that he had many gifts to give, but none to satisfy this particular list. Santa began feeling a little sad and a little bad. Then all of a sudden Santa began to smile.

You see, as powerful and good as Santa is, he fully knows there is one greater than he. Even Santa knows that the ultimate giver of good and perfect gifts does not dress in a red suit and hat.

Santa smiled contentedly.

He knew there was one who could give every gift on Phil's list. It would take a little help from Phil and the others on earth; but it could be done. If all the humans south of the North Pole would just get together with each other and the great gift-giver, every item on Phil's list could be checked off.

Santa knew it wouldn't be easy. But Santa knew things that many of us do not. Santa knew that the sky was his domain. He also knew there was one greater whose domain is the universe.

How about you? Are you willing to acknowledge and work together with your friends and family, and with the great gift-giver this Christmas to make Phil's list come true? Santa and Phil both hope so.

Now Santa, about that blue dial RGM 150 pilot watch? Do you think you could…??

Amen and Amen

A Premonition of Time

Some things defy understanding. Every once in a while in life, something so out of the ordinary happens that it makes us step back and reconsider what one does or does not know, especially about time.

I was reminded of this the other day as I was reading "I Rode with Stonewall" by Henry Kyd Douglas, a young staff member of Stonewall Jackson's during the Civil War. In the book he recounts an episode at the battle of Chancellorsville in 1863. He tells the story of the final hours of General E.F. Paxton, the commander of the Stonewall Brigade. Paxton had a terrific career and was so highly regarded he was given command of Jackson's old brigade once Stonewall was promoted. Paxton was a graduate of Washington College, Yale, and the University of Virginia. He was an attorney. He was bright, well-educated, and well respected. Here is the story, describing the situation at Chancellorsville in Douglas' own words:

> I found General Paxton very much depressed; he had been so for several days. We had a long conversation late at night. At the conclusion, he repeated what he had stated to me in the beginning, that he was convinced he would not survive the next day's battle. He did not seem morbid or superstitious but he spoke with earnest conviction. He then told me exactly where certain private and personal papers were to be found in his desk, then in his headquarters' wagon, and told me what some of them were. He requested me to see to it that they were not lost but sent to Lexington. He had the picture of his wife and his

Bible with him. He concluded by asking me to write to his wife as soon as he was killed and to see that his body was sent to Lexington by Cox, his faithful orderly, who had recently been made his aide-de-camp. I was never so impressed by a conversation in my life. Paxton was not an emotional man but one of strong mind, cool action, and great force of character. He was the last man to give way to a superstition. When he finished I had no doubt of his sincerity and of his awful prescience. (p. 224)

The next day, Paxton died of a bullet wound to his chest. He had been in many battles; this one was his last. Paxton had a premonition of his own death. Did that make the Union soldier's sharpshooter shoot straighter? Did it make Paxton more reckless? Did his understanding that his "time" was up, contribute to his death? The rational mind tries to make sense out of it.

It was the early 1970's. I was the English Pastor of a Chinese Baptist church near Los Angeles. I was working on my doctorate in the integration of theology and psychology. I was working at the church to support myself while in graduate school. One Saturday morning, the senior pastor called me at home, "Phil, can you please come see me in my office as soon as you can get here?" Being a young man of tremendous self-confidence, I immediately wondered what I had done wrong. I was totally unprepared for what I was about to hear.

Just a word about the pastor; he was one of the Godliest men I have ever known. He had been tortured during the Japanese invasion of China in the late thirties. He was brilliant. He had a doctorate degree in theology (as did his wife). He was a powerful preacher in three languages. I was privileged to serve under him. He taught me much. Within half an hour I was at the church. As I cautiously entered his office he said "Phil, I need to talk with you." He was so serious; I knew I was in trouble! "God has revealed to me during prayer this morning that I will die in the hospital next week; I will not survive my surgery," he stated calmly and quietly.

We all knew he was going into the hospital after church the next day for a routine gall bladder removal surgery. I immediately tried to reason with him and assure him that all would be well. He was adamant. He then proceeded to tell me what he wanted me to do upon his death. We had a complicated church. There were services in English, Mandarin, and Cantonese. We had a real mixture of old and young Chinese congregants. He was the glue that held it all together. He told me in great detail how I should work with the elders. He advised me to go to L.A. City College and take conversational Mandarin. The elderly would not accept me unless I showed some ability to converse with them in their own language. He then gave me a beautiful Bible. He calmly ushered me out, indicating he was going to stay and pray a while. I was in shock. I didn't know what to think. There I was, a doctoral student seeking to understand the interaction of psychology and theology; yet nothing in my course work had prepared me for that conversation.

Early Tuesday afternoon our senior pastor died.

He had massive internal bleeding. It was a routine surgery, yet he knew it was his "time." He met his heavenly father in his mid-sixties. He had not been sick one day in the years I had served under him. Today as I write this, I am older than he was when he died. I couldn't explain it then. I cannot explain it now. I still shudder when I think about it. How did he know? How did God "tell" him? Why doesn't God talk to me like that? Will I know when it is my time to die? What really is the linkage between the mind and the body? Could a premonition of death create massive bleeding in the abdomen?

As I said at the beginning of this homily, some things are past understanding. Time marches forward in equal segments for each one of us. Yet, somehow in some way, some few of us get tapped on the shoulder, reminded that our time is short. Some people are blessed with sensitivity to things that the rest of us cannot or do not know.

General Paxton and our pastor were two Godly men who lived and died to remind us to live life to the fullest while we have time. Scripture tells us that to everything there is a season . . . a time. May God grant each of us the wisdom to live however many seasons we are granted to the maximum. God knows the length of our time; He rarely lets us in on that. The finest chronometer in the world cannot tell any of us how much time is allotted to us.

My prayer for each of you is that you will make the most and the best of time, approaching life with a joyful abandon. Laugh; sing; dance; and love; the greatest of these is love.

Amen and Amen

A-One-of-a-Kind

Once upon a time a very loving family lived in a very cozy home. The house was so tiny, one big room served as kitchen, dining area and living room.

A beautiful grandfather (tall case) clock stood in one corner of the living room. It was wonderfully carved. It had a big booming chime. It was the tallest thing in the house. It was so tall, it could see across the small room to the kitchen area.

Staring back at it from the kitchen wall was a comfortable kitchen clock. This kitchen clock was white with red trim. It perched on a ledge above the stove. It wasn't tall. It did not boom. It basically buzzed. That's it . . . a barely bearable buzz. It got its power from a white cord attached to the nearest electrical outlet. The grandfather clock didn't like that kitchen clock. It wasn't sure why . . . but it just did not like that kitchen clock.

Every evening when the daddy came home from work, he carefully and lovingly placed his prize wristwatch on a wooden shelf near the bedroom door. He always remembered to wind it up before he set it down. Every evening he tenderly put it in its place on the shelf . . . face up . . . in plain sight of the kitchen clock. The kitchen clock didn't like that wristwatch. It wasn't sure why, but it just did not like that wristwatch.

One evening, the house grew quiet. The wristwatch settled in on its shelf for its long evening nap. It hoped they had forgotten to wind the big grandfather clock. It hated those booming boisterous chimes. They were so loud four times every hour from early morning till late at night. That big clock was such a show-off. The wristwatch really didn't like that grandfather clock. It wasn't sure why . . . but it just did not like that clock.

Every evening at 10:00 PM, the big clock in the living room sang its final song for the night. On this particular night, the wristwatch on the shelf had heard enough. "You are such a show-off," it cried out. "Why can't you ever just keep quiet? Everyone knows you're their favorite . . . so tall and handsome . . . so . . . so . . . tall and well-carved . . . so tall and such a big beautiful voice! I wish for one evening you would just hush and give us some peace and quiet and besides everyone knows you are their favorite!"

The grandfather clock was taken aback by the outburst. It was especially irritated at the chuckle coming from the kitchen clock. "What are you snickering at?" it growled, as it glared through the dim glow of the room. "Everyone knows you are their favorite," grumbling to that kitchen clock. "No one even notices when I chime; they are all so used to it. But every time that irritating little buzzer of yours goes off everyone comes a' running. The cookies are done; the pie is baked; the roast is cooked; oh yes, you are certainly their favorite! They never even notice me anymore."

It appeared that the tall grandfather clock slumped a bit as it bemoaned its loss of stature. The family always laughed and looked longingly at that kitchen clock. They were happy when its timer went off. Sweet smells drifted through the little house. No, the grandfather clock did not like that buzzardly buzzer one little bit. It knew that kitchen clock was their favorite.

The kitchen clock cried out to the wristwatch, "I don't know what you are complaining about! You don't have to hang here hearing that clock's horrible noise all day long! You are their favorite. We all know that. Why, father takes you with him everywhere. You get to travel all over." It bitterly buzzed, "It isn't fair; I see how he carefully winds you every evening. You get to go to exciting places and see the world. It just isn't fair! I never get to go anywhere. I just have to hang here hour after hour." All of a sudden, the kitchen clock didn't feel much like buzzing. It was very sad just hanging around the kitchen all the time. It knew that wristwatch was their favorite.

Three unhappy timepieces lived together in that little house. None of the three appreciated their unique place in the home. None of the three realized how it was prized by the family for its own special gift. Each clock was too busy wishing it was like the other to realize its own perfect place.

How about you? Has God blessed you with a special place in the world? Do you have a very important role to play in someone's life? Don't waste one minute of your precious time looking at others. Some of us are chimers, some of us busily buzz around, while others are just made to be quietly close to the one they love. Whatever your role, accept it as a gift from God. Be the best you can be at whomever you are and at whatever you do.

Find the purpose for which God has made you. Take a lesson from the clocks. Take a lesson from the Clockmaker. He has made you unique. You are not a limited edition . . . you are a one-of-a-kind!

Amen and Amen

An Olympics of a Different Kind

The Olympics are just around the corner. I am confident that this or that watch company will pay a zillion dollars for the rights to be the official timer.

The successful company will not run, jump, or compete in the contests. It will however be readily displayed as it tracks the quickest times, the elapsed times, or the time limits for many events. It will be the winner's best friend and the loser's worst enemy. Time will pass too quickly for those who are behind and too slowly for those in the lead. Only one thing is for sure; it will pass. Each of us would like time to be at our mercy, yet it rarely heeds our call.

It is almost inevitable in sports and typing; we look for the fastest time with the fewest errors. We watch for world record times. To the quick goes the gold.

This year I want to suggest a different kind of Olympics. Perhaps some great watch company will agree to sponsor it. Timing will be crucial. In my Olympics the rewards will go to the slowest. The hesitant will get the bronze. The reluctant will win silver. The slowest will win the gold.

I think the world would be a better place this summer if we would reward:

- The slow to fight
- The slow to speak (especially when they have nothing to say)
- The slow to anger

Let's honor those who are:

- Hesitant to strike back
- Hesitant to deflect responsibility
- Hesitant to take joy in their enemy's loss

Let's give the winner's crown to those who:

- Put standing on principle above standing on a podium
- Put exercising restraint above exercising muscles
- Put the pursuit of peace above the pursuit of glory
- Turn the other cheek, knowing their face is going to hurt

May we be slow:

- To have to be right
- To have to be first
- To have to be best

May we be quick to realize:

- When someone wins, most everyone else loses
- Triumph comes in being **your** best; not in being **the** best
- Being good isn't as important as being faithful
- Rush hour is really the slowest time of the day
- Never falling isn't the goal; getting up each time you fall makes you the winner
- If you rush through life, you will miss the joy of the journey.

I am all for a different kind of Olympics; will anyone else join me?
Amen and Amen

Happy New Year's Day! –
Finding a New Center

The New Year breaks through time once a year in the same way the sun pierces the darkness every morning. Indeed our fascination with watches and time reflects our linear understanding of the cycles of our lives. We have neatly divided our chronological experience into even increments: seconds, minutes, hours, days, months, years, decades, and so on. It is all very tidy. There are minimal variances (such as leap years) in our chronological sequences. As watch nuts, some of us are fanatic about these sequences to the point of timing our watches for variances in the range of seconds per day. It is all orderly and predictable.

It is also terribly impersonal. Nothing that happens to us or by us alters the inevitable movement of time as we understand and experience it. Time moves in sequences that are beyond us and over which we have little or no control. Time moves on whether I wind my watch or not. At any point, the failure of my watch to register the passage of time has no impact on its inevitable movement. My watch has as little impact on the passage of time as we know it, as the sails of a ship do the wind.

Not all cultures have such a tidy template for time. Many indigenous people tie time to events. Last year might not be identified by a numerical sequence (2006) but would be understood as the time of the tsunami, the time the twins were born, or the time I broke my leg. In this concept, time is directly tied to events that shape lives or are created by the participant-observer. Gone is time's impersonal nature. Exactitude is not the valued feature. A link, tie-in, or purpose to and for the observer is what is valued.

For the Pueblo groups of the American Southwest the understanding of events and time is organized around the concept of "centers." Centers are not linear or sequential. They are messy. They intersect and overlap in the fullness of life. Instead of organizing existence around the movement of the sun, moon, and planets, life is understood and organized around the physical, environmental, and spiritual/emotional centers that combine together at any one time to impact life.

Dr. Rina Swentzell, a Santa Clara Pueblo born writer believes that we in Western culture are vaguely aware of the concept of centers, but also that "rationalism became highly valued in the West, and with it came an adherence to the idea of linear time, in which place and experience do not intersect in a multidimensional way."

The most important center in the Puebloan understanding of time and events is the *bupingeh*. Dr. Swentzell defines the Tewa concept of *bupingeh* as the *"center heart place."* For the Tewa, the *bupingeh* focuses on the events, relationships, people, and buildings of the home, family, and local community. It is the center where the most intimate physical, emotional and spiritual events and feelings occur and intertwine. It is messy; a place and time where life happens at its deepest and most profound level. Atomic clocks and watches are of little value in the *center heart place*.

I love the concept of the family, home, and community as the *bupingeh* or *center heart place* through which the most important feelings, events and times flow. It is a place that deserves our very special attention and focus. The steady rhythm of time is important, but so much more that which forms the true meaning and significance of our lives.

In our understanding of time, this is New Year's Day. Please also make it a time to recommit to your own *bupingeh* or *center heart place*. Make it the place of peace. If you do, you may never think of time in the same way again. ***Amen and Amen***

The Heavenly Horologist

There seems to be a lot of talk about spirituality or the lack thereof these days. This is especially true when discussing how faith intersects life. *The Da Vinci Code* and *Angels and Demons* are runaway best sellers. *The Guide to the Da Vinci Code* and *The Guide to Angels and Demons* are best sellers. *The Guide to the Guide to the Da Vinci Code* and *The Guide to the Guide to Angels and Demons* will soon be best sellers. Red versus blue states; Republican versus Democrat values . . . Terry Schiavo . . . the pope's death . . . Islamic values versus Western culture and values (or the lack thereof). Never in my sixty plus years have I seen such an interest in the role religion, faith, science, values, etc. play in real life. While Dan Brown's books certainly don't portray real life, they are phenomena that cannot be ignored.

Alongside the expected works by John Grisham and Dan Brown, this week's NY Times bestseller list includes a work called *The Rising* by Tim LaHaye and Jerry Jenkins. No one outside of evangelicalism has ever heard of Jerry Jenkins. He is a ghost writer for such people as Billy Graham (and obviously Tim LaHaye). Tim LaHaye is most noted among evangelicals for being 110 years old (slight exaggeration) and for having memorized the entire New Testament. I can remember, as a boy looking at him with awe and wonder as he challenged anyone to reference any New Testament verse (I John 1:9, for example). No matter how obscure the verse he would immediately quote the verse in its entirety, regardless of its obscurity. That was quite a feat given the fact that there are 7,957 verses in the New Testament. Now he is a best-selling author. While this interest seems unprecedented for our times, it is not new.

William Paley was an eighteenth-century Anglican priest/scholar who wrote prolifically on the very same issues. Faced with the skepticism of the Enlightenment, people were trying their best to figure out how faith fit into life. Paley's famous argument revolved around a watch! He argued that if one was strolling across a British moor and found a pocket watch in the dirt, running and telling the right time, the appropriate conclusion would be that a watchmaker had indeed made the watch. His argument from "design" became a leading postulate for the existence of God that is still quoted today; certainly something as complicated as a watch implied a watchmaker; something as complicated as the universe implied a universe maker. Paley's conclusion was that the universe/watchmaker was God. Darwin studied Paley's argument for the existence of God from the world's design, but rejected them for his own conclusions.

This horological defense of the existence of God has had such an impact on conservatives over the years that Richard Dawkins, a modern day Oxford Professor of Public Understanding of Science wrote a book entitled, *The Blind Watchmaker,* the purpose of which is to posit that evolution is indeed the blind watchmaker of the universe. Over hundreds of millions of years, natural selection refined and defined creation until the appearance of design came about. Paley, the eighteenth century theologian and Dawkins, the twenty-first century biologist, through their writings still engage in this horological hassle.

Another version of the God-as-watchmaker debate reared its head in eighteenth and nineteenth century deism. Deism was also a reaction to the Enlightenment. It was an attempt to reconcile God with advances in science. Borrowing from Paley's metaphor, the deist taught that God was indeed a heavenly horologist. He had created the world-watch, wound it up, stood back with benevolent pride, and let the watch run. Natural laws took over once creation was complete. God did not need to tweak or time the watch-world. He designed it to perfection, sat back in his heavenly hammock and watched (no pun intended) it run. It was the perfect solution to the science versus faith debate of that time. Scientists of the time were beginning to understand the laws of entropy, so they were afraid the world-watch was running down. Therefore, more debate ensued. What would be the result when the world-watch mainspring ran down? Would the watchmaker wade back in, winding it all back up again? No one knew for sure. Of course, that lack of certainty never stopped either eighteenth and nineteenth scientists or polemicists from confidently strutting their stuff.

Hundreds of years later the debate rages on in both fact and fiction. Would scientists really like to blow up the Vatican? Would the Vatican really like to blow up the scientists? Are Republicans Godlier than Democrats? Will non-Christians ever see heaven? Is there a heaven? How does faith intersect with death? Why do Muslims dislike the West? Do they? Is there a right to life? Is there a right to death? What about choice including the choice to live or to die? Church versus state? Red versus blue? Scientific facts versus faith? Progress versus loneliness? Isolation versus community? The debates go on and on. Is God the Watchmaker who designs and creates; the Watchmaker who fixes and repairs? Or is He the result of our needs for something greater than ourselves? Is He the human-created fixer-upper who gives us confidence amidst our doubts and certainties amidst our confusion?

Different people come to different conclusions on these questions. My thoughts today are more on the process of the inquiry, rather than its conclusion:

- Enter into these discussions with humility. You don't have to be arrogant.
- Enter into these discussions with kindness. You don't have to be mean.
- Enter into these discussions with uncertainty. You don't have all the answers.

- Enter into these discussions with appreciation. You might just learn something.
- Enter into these discussions realizing that life's experiences have painted a different picture for each of us. Try to understand the palette, paint, and paper of the other's life and how each has impacted and framed all of our views, perspectives, and identity.
- Enter into these discussions with a certainty that some things are uncertain. You don't have to be sure of everything.
- Enter into these discussions caring for the other person as much as you care for your position. You don't have to be cold.
- Enter into these discussions knowing that God is God. You are not.

Watches are beautiful and functional machines. Their hundreds of parts work together for a common purpose. Let us commit to being more like our watches. Let us each do our part to make the whole work; with humility and gratitude for the role we play in each other's lives. We are each a vital component of the world in which we live. Whether or not you acknowledge the role of a Watchmaker in your life, please live as if you are vital to the person next to you, and they to you, regardless of the presence or absence of the same outlook on life. Ralph Waldo Emerson gave us a good reminder, "Let me never fall into the vulgar mistake of dreaming that I am persecuted whenever I am contradicted."

Amen and Amen

Koinonia: The Fellowship of the Forum

Well, it is 2:21 am Sunday here in Florida. I am watching the Nigeria-Argentina soccer match. I lived and traveled on the border between Nigeria and Dahomey (Benin) as a young man. It is therefore, one of my adopted countries. It is also Sunday and time for my weekly horological homily.

I am tremendously impressed by the wonderful spirit of enthusiasm and fellowship generated among the members of this forum related to the EOT-1. (The forum referred to was a watch collecting forum on which I was a regular. The EOT-1 referred to a watch that was being designed by consensus among members of the forum and which would be built by the RGM watch company of Lititz, PA, the primary sponsor of the forum. I still own the final product. It is a simple yet wonderful watch.)

Both concepts, enthusiasm and fellowship are the subject of today's homily. Enthusiasm comes from the Greek term *en Theos* - in God. Enthusiasm in its literal classical sense was a passion generated from a sense of spirituality. I want to focus, however, on the concept of fellowship. Ever since joining this forum, I have been impressed by the sense of fellowship present here.

In Greek, the word for fellowship is *koinonia*. It comes from the root word *koine* meaning common. The language of the everyday Greek citizen was called *koine* Greek or "common" Greek. *Koinonia* was a term that referred to a group of people who had something specific in common. It often took on a spiritual sense, but not always. Peter, James, and John - all eventual disciples were *en koinonia*, translated *partners* in their fishing business.

The EOT1 - Fellowship in the Forum (Photo by the Author)

I am amazed at all that the members of this forum have in common with each other.

1. A sense of enjoyment of and fun with each other.

2. A mutual respect for each other's thoughts and opinions.

3. A welcoming of newcomers and returning old friends.

4. A non-judgmental approach to each other.

5. A willingness to share information and knowledge.

6. A genuine concern for each other's well-being.

7. A certain 36mm watch, both in the designing and the wearing.

8.   A joy in sharing all things related to watches.

Are we a church? Not hardly. Do we exhibit the characteristics of true fellowship? Yes, in so many ways. I commend this forum for its spirit of *koinonia* -- fellowship in its truest form -- having so many things in common. Koinonia may be a great name for our next collaboration watch? It would be a watch demonstrating and reflective of the fellowship of a bunch of watch enthusiasts who have found they have much more in common. Maybe, just maybe there is a lesson in there to for some churches!

Amen and Amen

A Haunting Tale!

Previously I have told the reader about the collaborative effort on the EOT Watch Forum to design a watch based on the input from all forum members. After several months, we had a watch that was called the *EOT-1 Collaboration*. You all have seen the photo of the beautiful watch on a previous homily. Rich, the marketing and public relations guy for the RGM Watch Company wanted to make a beautiful image of the watch that would be appropriate as wallpaper on a desktop computer. For that purpose I lent him a beautiful book whose front cover had many images of instruments that were precursors to our modern watches, telescopes, and the like. He created the image and one of our members, John was the first to use it for wallpaper on his computer monitor. John told us all how amazing it looked. And now the rest of the story . . .

Following John's lead I made Rich's scan my wallpaper in Windows. It stretched out to a huge, virtually perfect picture. It was very, very nice. The watch is quite large and the overall effect is stunning.

Last night I was working well past midnight in my office. At one point I minimized a browser window to move to something else. I swear (as much as a homiletics professor swears) that out of the corner of my eye I saw the hands moving on the EOT-1 staring at me from the monitor. There, as plain as midnight, the second hand was moving in perfect motion. It really grabbed my attention. Then, after I focused on it, I realized it was perfectly still. A possessed watch residing on a former seminarian's computer that just wouldn't do!

I opened the browser and routinely checked another forum. I found a reply to an inquiry I had made about German watches. Someone indicated that a Ranier Neinaber makes great German watches.

Never having heard of him, I did a Google search and voila there was his home page. I clicked on the link, found his home page, and then clicked on his clock page. Just as it was loading, the urge hit, so I left my desk to go to the office restroom. I minimized the window and left.

When I came back I was astonished. My EOT-1 had started ticking! There it was, big, beautiful, and now ticking! I could swear the second hand was moving and more than that, it was loudly and clearly ticking. I pulled out the cross from my neck chain, gripped it in my hand, and approached the computer!

No doubt about it; it was ticking! Now, I knew I was either working much too late or Beelzebub himself had invaded my EOT-1.

Yes, my friends it was ticking. The minimized Ranier Neinaber clock site, that is, was ticking away through my computer speakers. Nice sound effects Ranier, you about scared the few years I have left right out of me!

After maximizing his site, I quickly clicked on the X up in the right hand corner (an ancient exorcism rite I learned in seminary). The ticking stopped. The sanctity of my office slowly returned. I stayed there till about 1:30 a.m., every ten minutes or so warily minimizing my work to glance at the eerie EOT-1 emanating into the evening. There was no further movement of the hands and no ticking from the speakers!

Now I remember; to take the picture, Rich put the EOT-1 on top of the book I lent him. It was the biography of Tycho Brahe, the famous Danish astronomer and instrument maker. His observatory on Sven Island in Denmark was eventually shut down by local people who thought demonic things were going on there. After having trained map and instrument greats like Willem Blaeu and Gerardus Mercator, Brahe barely escaped with his life. Hmm . . . maybe they knew something! Hmm . . . I wonder? *Amen and Amen*

Jumping into the Hole

I first heard the following story on an episode of "The West Wing." This past week I was reminded of it.

This guy is walking down the street when he falls in a hole. The walls are so steep he can't get out. A doctor passes by and the guy shouts up, "Hey you! Can you help me out?" The doctor writes a prescription, throws it down in the hole, and moves on.

Then a priest comes along and the guy shouts up, "Father, I'm down in this hole, can you help me out?" The priest writes out a prayer, throws it down in the hole, and moves on.

Then a friend walks by. "Hey, Joe, it's me can you help me out?" Then the friend jumps in the hole. Our guy says, "Are you stupid? Now we're both down here." The friend says, "Yeah, but I've been down here before and I know the way out."

Last Sunday I wrote a homily dealing with fellowship. This week with your lives and generosity, you collectively wrote a homily dealing with fellowship.

This week a group of guys showed what they truly have in common; the willingness to jump in the hole to help a friend. I can say nothing more eloquent than that. You didn't give advice. You didn't write a prescription or a prayer. Many of you dug into your pockets and gave. You didn't give advice or opinion, but of your own money.

This week many of you jumped in the hole with one of our forum friends. I salute you for that. I salute you for caring enough to give. I salute the members of this amazing forum. Collectively, you *are* this week's horological homily. ***Amen and Amen***

When Time Stands Still

I have been doing a lot of research lately on the civil war. I am writing a work of historical fiction that is set in part during the war. Naturally, when in the course of during my research, I see something about watches, it catches my attention:

1. Did you know the Waltham watch company made the first ever "made for a lady" watch in 1861? Many women in the north were going into the workplace and they demanded a watch made for them. Waltham (then the American Watch Company) obliged and made the first ladies watch.

2. Did you know that before the war, Ulysses S. Grant was so poor that he pawned his prize heirloom pocket watch in order to buy his children Christmas presents?

3. Remember Wild Bill Hickok? Did you know he was a union scout during the civil war? For his service, he was given a prized pocket watch. After the war, during a poker game in Springfield, Missouri Wild Bill lost the watch. He then discovered that his opponent had cheated. Wild Bill confronted his opponent in an old-fashioned duel. His opponent was killed. Wild Bill took back his watch and went on to fame. By the way, his opponent's gravestone in Springfield has an engraved pocket watch on it!

Speaking of time, on some occasions it seems to "fly." Why did the man put his watch on his pet parrot? He wanted to see time fly! Yet, on some occasions it simply seems to stand still. Time may seem to slow down to a crawl or even completely stop. I had such an experience last week. I moved into a time warp. A week ago Monday I found myself back 138 years in time. I wasn't in church, but it was truly a spiritual experience.

A little-known event occurred on December 9, 1864 about twenty-one miles north of Savannah, Georgia. Sherman was marching through Georgia. One-half of his army followed the old Augusta road south along the Savannah River towards the city of Savannah. Thousands of slaves had joined the army's procession south. They were newly freed and looking for protection from the union troops. The slave men worked as "pioneers" clearing the roads for the troops. The women, children, and elderly followed behind the troops. It is said that the Union Army commanding officer General Jefferson Davis (yes that was his name) was miffed by the slave's presence. They slowed him down and needed fed. By the time they reached a badly swollen and flooded Ebenezer Creek (150 feet across and 20 feet deep in flood stage), it is estimated there were between 2,000 and 10,000 slaves following the troops.

Davis ordered a pontoon bridge built across the swollen river (the Confederate soldiers had destroyed the only bridge). The troops passed over. The slaves were held back. Immediately when the last soldier was across, Davis ordered the bridge to be taken up. His plan was to strand the slaves on the other side of the creek, thus freeing his army of them. The slaves panicked. They panicked even more when the confederate General Wheeler and his cavalry charged them. Wheeler had been harassing the troops every step of the way from Atlanta. Hundreds of slaves poured into the icy river trying to escape Wheeler. Many drowned. Many were killed by the Confederate troops. Many were captured and returned to their masters. Union officers were horrified as they watched from the opposite shore. Many tried to help. It is estimated that at least 600 slaves died that day. One Union officer said the bodies were so thick; they formed a dam across the river.

It was a terrible loss of life and a horrible tragedy. The Union Army blamed Wheeler. Wheeler blamed Davis. Word of the event got to Washington via horrified union officers. Secretary of War Stanton was dispatched to Savannah to find out the truth from Sherman, who had been approximately twenty miles away at the time of the tragedy. No one in either army was ever censured or disciplined.

Today, the old Augusta road is gone. No bridge was ever rebuilt over the creek. The site of the tragedy (massacre, disaster - you pick the word) is miles from any access. There are no roads and no trails, just primitive swamp lands. The only way to get there is by canoe or other small boat. There are lots of gators and snakes.

Last week my wife and I went to Ebenezer Creek. We hiked and canoed to the very spot of the Ebenezer Creek massacre. Utter silence. Utter stillness. No people. No roads. No vehicles. Never had I experienced so many sensations in the presence of such stillness. Magnificent cypress and tall pines, naked for at least fifty feet high dotted the landscape. Moss, symbolizing the weeping of the trees at what they had seen so many years ago, hung on the trees. We couldn't help but weep as well. For a few brief hours I didn't need my trusty Schwarz Etienne wristwatch because for those hours, time stood still. At a minimum, hundreds of people died that day on that spot, yet until 2010 no marker hallowed their memory. The episode was so controversial; few civil war books even mention it. Nothing but the beauty of God's creation serves to sanctify the spot. Prejudice is a terrible thing. People owning people is a terrible thing. Hate is a terrible thing.

The trip to the spot of the Ebenezer Creek Massacre was a sad event for us. Far sadder however is what happened when we got back to civilization. Returning the canoe, we stopped for lunch at a restaurant near the boat landing. We were obviously strangers. While eating we struck up conversation with a local fellow sitting across from us. When we told him where we had been and why, he smirked. I will never forget that smirk. He said to us, "I don't want to sound prejudiced, but I wish they'd killed all them n.......s that day. We'd all be better off if they'd killed them all." I wanted to hit him.

My stomach turned sick as I realized that in the most tragic way, for that man, time had indeed stood still. I think it was the saddest thing anyone has ever said to me. The tragedy at Ebenezer Creek was a terrible event. It was the result of the ignorance, fears, prejudice, and hate of the middle of the nineteenth century. Unfortunately, it seems that in some hearts and minds all of that is still with us.

Let me encourage each of you to search your own hearts and minds. Root out the seeds of prejudice, meanness, and bias. Thinking less of a fellow human because of his or her faith, skin color, ethnicity, or heritage is a terrible thing.

Maybe none of you will ever travel to Ebenezer Creek in Georgia. But you will go to work, school, or church. You will interact with people in your communities. Please treat your fellow human beings as you would want treated. That is, after all the golden rule. It is the ultimate homily. Yes, it is even the ultimate horological homily because time never runs out on the need for us to practice kindness and respect to everyone.

Amen and Amen

Who Winds the Watch in the Midst of the Winds?

Living through two hurricanes in three weeks, expecting a third, and experiencing damage, destruction, and despair leads one to the examination of values as well as of what is valuable. One's destiny, the sovereignty of God, fatalism, punishments, blessings, natural causes, supernatural intervention, and dumb luck all receive scrutiny in such a time. Perhaps the primary question in these moments is, "Who Winds the Watch in the Midst of the Winds?"

Down the street from my home, a very devout veterinarian always posts scripture verses on his sign. This week's verse states boldly, "He brings rain on the just and the unjust," a rather loose translation of part of Matthew 5:45. Yesterday, a local reporter interviewed a family. They stated that God's blessing kept them safe in the midst of the storm. As I watched, I wondered about the implications of that statement on those who had lost everything or who had been hurt in the same storm. If being kept safe was a divine blessing, what was losing all, a punishment, divine curse, dumb luck, or simple fate?

Questions regarding the winding of the watch have intrigued humans for centuries. Is the world like a quartz watch, charged by some divine battery and left to run untended for years? This was the belief of the deists, amply represented among America's founding fathers. God created and then allowed His laws to carry out His purposes. Storms were the results of interactions of nature, all set in motion by the Divine and then left to run their own course. Rarely did God intervene in the world He had created. Prayer was for the pray-er. It soothed and consoled but rarely changed anything.

Is the world like a mechanical watch, needing periodic winding or shaking by a divine hand? The ancient Greeks and Romans used the concept of "deus ex machina" in their dramas. When their plays reached a pivotal point of crisis, a crane would drop a god figure into the action. This god would then decide the outcome. Is such periodic divine intervention the winding that keeps the watch ticking on for hours and days on its own? Is the storm in the night such an intervention?

The sixteenth and seventeenth century puritans saw the intervention of the divine in the jeremiad. The term "jeremiad" is taken from the Lamentations of Jeremiah, one of the books of the Old Testament. The jeremiad is the result of the benevolent judgment of God. Lest you think that is a contradiction in terms, hear me out. In the puritan view of the world, when humans made things go awry, God would intervene with judgment, not for the purpose of punishment as an end in itself. The purpose of the punishment was purification, a return to God brought on by suffering, repentance and confession. The end result was superior to the beginning condition. The chain of events in a jeremiad goes something like this: humans sin, God judges, humans repent (the Greek word metanoia, means "turn around"), humans mend their ways, God blesses, things are better than ever. Thus natural disasters, diseases, etc. are a jeremiad, an intervention by God designed to bring about purification. God intervenes to make everything ultimately better. The vision is of the homeowner, who loses all, realizes how misplaced his or her values were, becomes more focused on family and simplicity, and moves to a better place than before the suffering of the storm.

The naturalist or skeptic believes the world is more like a sundial. The sundial needs little or no intervention to tell the time. Clouds may obscure the time for a time, but all is natural. The divine may or may not exist in some form, theory, principle, person, or system of beliefs. None of that matters to the sundial. Once a person learns the science, the technology of the sundial, he or she is able to tell the time as well as anyone else. Storms come and go, easily explained by the science of meteorology, angles, cause, and effect. If the storm track isn't quite right (as with Charley), more and better science is the need. Steering currents are the focus, not philosophical introspection.

If I pray to God for the storm to avoid Sarasota and it goes somewhere else wreaking pain and death is that to be interpreted as a result of my prayer? I shudder to think that may be the case. Not wanting to inflict pain on anyone else, for what then do I pray? Do I pray that I should learn all I can from the storm (the jeremiad)? Do I pray for strength to endure the loss? Do I pray at all, or is my time better spent watching Jim Harrigan, channel seven's chief meteorologist?

Perhaps the greatest speech ever given by an American president was the second inaugural speech of Abraham Lincoln. It also was one of the shortest. It was certainly one of the most theological-centric speeches given in public by a sitting president. In the center portion of the speech, speaking of the North and South, Lincoln states, "Both read the same Bible, and pray to the same God; and each invokes His aid against the other. . . . The prayers of both could not be answered; that of neither has been answered fully. The Almighty has his own purposes."

Not a trained theologian or philosopher, perhaps Lincoln has answered the watch-winding question the best. Perhaps the best answer reflects the greatest humility. The Almighty has His own purposes. If He created the wind, He can allow it to blow according to the laws of His nature. Or He can intervene. It is His choice according to His purpose.

What then should I do? I must **prepare**. I must **protect**. And yes, I can **pray**. For what should I pray? I still am not sure, but I think I must pray that the purpose of God be lived out in whatever happens and that I am the very best instrument of that purpose that I can be. I may experience stress, but certainly no more than that of the mainspring when wound by the hand of the watchmaker. Life is full of winds: fair, balmy, breezy, stormy and yes, even hurricane. May I embrace each, seeking to always better and more completely understand the hand of Him who winds the watch in the midst of the winds.

Amen and Amen

I am grateful to Ronald White, Jr, author of the fine book, *Lincoln's Greatest Speech: The Second Inaugural*, and to Hurricanes Charley and Frances for many of the thoughts and illustrations that inspired this homily.

Just in Time

The English language is full of idioms. Some of them involve the word "time":

- Just in time
- A hard time
- A dickens of a time
- Big time
- Bad time
- Keeping up with the times
- Tough times

I am sure there are many others. These are the ones that come to my mind *at this time*. But *time's up* and I have to get this homily done *on time*. I can't spend any *more time wasting time* trying to think of more, so I will *call time-out* and be done. *Time flies* and soon it will be Sunday and then *time will be up*! If you have enough *time on your hands* to be reading this, you probably have *time to kill*. Ok! Ok! I will stop. I guess you get the point. Some of you got it in *no time at all!* (Sorry)

Idioms are combinations of words that make sense to native speakers, but can be quite confusing when spoken to non-natives. Every language has idioms. I remember one time in Los Angeles I was preaching to a Mandarin congregation. I spoke in English and my interrupter as I called him, interpreted into Mandarin. Twice in one sermon I used idioms that caused him real grief. I said to the congregation "I am not pulling your leg." Then later I said, "Some of you may think I am all wet." My faithful translator knew what I meant, he groaned and the English speakers laughed. I learned to try not to use idioms when speaking through an interrupter.

When I lived in Africa I learned the challenges that Bible translators face. How do you translate "washing your sins white as snow" in sub-Saharan Africa? As a seventeen year old, I once spoke in a little church on the Pacific coast of Mexico. Trying to give the announcements to the congregation in Spanish, I mixed up the word servicio (service) and cerveza (beer). Boy did that congregation laugh because I had just invited them back next week for another "beer." They were sure the church would be full!

Words do matter. Whoever wrote the phrase "Sticks and stones may break my bones but words will never hurt me" never grew up skinny and un-coordinated with lots of zits. In my years of counseling families I heard two time-related words that almost always hurt the recipient. They were "never" and "always."

- "She never tells me she loves me"
- "He never helps around the house"
- "He always comes home late for dinner"
- "She always mocks me"
- "He is always on my case"
- "She never tells me how she really feels"
- "He never obeys me"

"Always" and "Never" – two time related words that have more power than the largest sticks and stones. Words do matter. Catch yourself next time you find yourself saying "you always" or "you never." Usually we use these words in anger and as an expression of hurt. Be very careful in your use of these two horologically-related words. Save them for those rare occasions when they are true. If you can learn to make better use of these two words, you will **never** regret it. You will **always** be better for it!

Well it is almost Sunday so *time's up*!!! Whew, I'm done, just in the *nick of time*! ***Amen and Amen***

The Silent Servant

Joseph, husband of Mary and father of Jesus has always been my very favorite Biblical character. Whether or not you accept the Biblical account of the child's birth, you must admire Joseph. His bride-to-be was pregnant, an extremely rare occurrence in a strict first century Jewish society. Throughout all the account of their engagement, the birth of the child, the flight into Egypt and the raising/nurturing of his family, Joseph was faithful. He was also silent. I really like that about him. Throughout the gospels he is mentioned numerous times. Yet, in that same writing, there is no record of a single word he ever said. He is shown as being . . . not talking. I like that. No long sermons . . . no words of wisdom . . . just quiet calm strength in the face of tremendous adversity. Joseph and Mary had other children. They raised their family under some extraordinary conditions. Through it all he was a silent servant. We learn about him from what he did and who he was, not from what he said.

Only twice in the whole New Testament is the Greek word *tekton* (pronounced teck-tone) used. Both times it is used to describe Joseph's profession. In most English versions it is simply translated "carpenter." That is however, a very inadequate translation. Images of Joseph in Christianity almost invariably show him as the rough carpenter.

It is actually a wonderful word. Being a "tekton" did involve having some carpentry skills. In classical Greek it is used of builders . . . designers of great buildings. It often refers to what we call the "architect." (see the hidden word there?) The "tekton" might have been the contractor, the one who could organize the whole of the construction. He knew the intricacies of the entire design, literally the "technology" (Aren't words wonderful?) of the construction.

Yes, our word technology comes from the same Greek root word! Joseph was the first identified "technician." Shall I go on?

I like the word even more because it also was used in Greek to refer to a poet or an artist who had elevated his or her craft to the highest degree. It was used of the very best songwriters. Almost anyone who took their craft to the highest form was known as a "tekton."

The Beauty of the Art of Roland Murphy of RGM Watches

What does this have to do with watches? Well, I think in the Greek word "tekton" I have discovered what separates average watchmakers from the great ones. How can I best describe the Roland Murphys and the Dirk Dornblueths? I would assign them the rank of the "tekton" of modern watchmakers. They are able to take steel and machine and blend them into a poem, a symphony of a watch. They elevate the craft of horology above their peers. I am sure there are many others. Roland and Dirk are the two whose work I personally enjoy the most. In small shops they serve as the architects of great watches. I appreciate the care, the time, the passion and the skill they put into their watches. They are, in my opinion the songwriters, the "tektons" of their craft.

How about you? Strive to put the music into whatever it is you do. Take the palette of your God-given skills and paint . . . paint . . . paint. Don't settle for being the carpenter. Work hard and hone your craft, whatever that may be, to become the very best . . . the "tekton" of your profession. Speaking of that, what exactly was Joseph's profession? Well, we don't fully know. Probably he was a master builder, an architect with the highest skills for his time. He was, in the Greek "ta tekton" of his craft.

I encourage each of you; let others see you for what you do and for who you are. Keep your words to a minimum. Be faithful in all you attempt. And while you are at it, write some music at work tomorrow. Paint a canvas with your labors. You can do it. You too can be like Joseph, Roland, and Dirk. You can be "ta tekton."

Amen and Amen

Making Time

It was August 1969. I was 20 years old. I had just spent a wonderful summer living in the "bush" in Benin in West Africa. No electricity, no running water, hunting for meat. It had been an exhilarating experience. Now it was time to go home. I left my little village with a sigh.

In Monrovia, Liberia I teamed up with a friend who attended the same university in Arkansas. We flew to London. He had a first cousin living there. We were to stay in London for several days to see the sites. I remember being so amazed at the memorials to the London Blitz. Lots of people we met had many memories of the terrible bombing.

We were to be in London over a weekend. My friend and I decided to go visit All Souls Church. All Souls was pastored by John R.W. Stott. John Stott was a hero to young divinity students in those years. He was the most influential evangelical theologian/pastor of the generation. His books were required reading in every theological curriculum. His name was heard in hushed whispers in the hallowed halls of homiletic heroes.

We determined to visit All Souls to hear "the man." The service was great; Stott was eloquent. It was all I hoped it would be. Being one of 2,000 attendees that morning made us both feel that we had touched our hero. After the service, we were quite surprised to see that Dr. Stott was standing at the door of the church, greeting his congregants as they filed out. Maybe there was a chance we could actually shake his hand! That would send waves of jealousy through the hearts of the homiletic hotshots back at school.

We did our best to work toward the door. We gently pushed and pulled our way toward the object of our attention. Finally we were there. Dr. Stott smiled a big smile at us and shook our hands. He asked us if we were visiting. Did he really know everyone in his congregation of thousands? We quickly explained we were American students on our way home. We told him we had studied his books and had appreciated them. We were thrilled. He was so gracious. Time stood still for two minutes while he chatted with us. Realizing that the line was growing, we knew it was time to move on. It was quite exciting for two young divinity students.

Before we left Dr. Stott, he smiled and said "Would you mind standing over there for a few minutes? I am a bit busy right now, but I would like to talk more with you." Would we wait???? Would we wait???? Of course we would wait; all day if necessary.

We watched Dr. Stott greet every single person who came through the line. It was more than a few minutes. We felt awkward but we were not budging. One of his associates came over and chatted with us in a most gracious manner.

Finally everyone had left. An assistant helped Dr. Stott out of his robe. He strolled over to us with a big smile and said in a wonderful British accent, "It's settled then; you're coming to my home for Sunday dinner." We couldn't believe our ears. Had he just asked us to have dinner with him? We must have misunderstood. No, we hadn't. We walked next door to the parsonage with him. We sat at the dinner table with him and three of his associates. John Stott was a bachelor. His housekeeper served a wonderful meal. We were so nervous we could hardly eat. He chatted with us before dinner, during dinner, and afterwards. He devoted almost his entire Sunday afternoon to us; just the two of us. We were skinny, shy American students who he had never met. He made us feel ten feet tall. He not only spent the afternoon with us, he made us feel important. He asked us our thoughts about things. He never once lectured us. He never once told us how things were. He mentored us, probing our future plans. He encouraged us in every way. It was one of the highlights of my life.

When we left late that afternoon, he gave us each a copy of one of his books. He autographed them for us. He thanked us for spending our afternoon with him. Can you believe that? He thanked us! Needless to say, we were thrilled. We told that story over and over back in school. To skeptical eyes we showed our books. We were the heroes of our dorms. Other students started asking us what we thought about things. It was a great feeling.

I am now 67 years old. I still have that book.

Over the years I have owned and read hundreds of books. That signed copy of *Basic Christianity* is still the most special book I have ever owned. Beyond the wisdom contained in its pages, it has taught me much more. During my years as professor, pastor, and dean, it sat on my desk. It reminded to make time.

I had been given a role model in Dr. Stott. I did my best to give everyone who crossed my path the time and the personal interest that Dr. Stott had given me. I know I failed many times. I am not by nature an outgoing and gracious person. Based on that wonderful Sunday afternoon in August 1969, I have tried to do my best.

How about you? Do you put as much time into making time as you do telling time? There are many people you encounter every day. Give them time. Make their day. Serve as a role model to those who look up to you. You don't have to be a hero to make a heroic impact.

Making time is more important than telling time.

Amen and Amen

The Broken Balance

Tomorrow I am going to the Orlando Watch Show. Just the thought of that brings back memories of last year. One minute I was the proud owner of a new Howard pocket watch. The next, it slipped out of my hands. Crashing to the concrete, it stopped running. I broke the balance staff. Five minutes of ownership and I had broken it. Hopefully tomorrow I will do better.

The balance, balance staff, and balance cock are integral to a watch's functioning. Together it is said they form the *controlling device* of the watch. When the balance of the watch is out of whack, the watch no longer runs correctly. It is no longer reliable. It no longer serves the purpose for which it was made.

So it is with life.

The Navajos call it *hozho*. *Hozho* is the state of living when all things are in harmony in one's life. The best single English translation is the word "balance." The Navajos believe when we have balance in all areas of our lives, we will be at peace, at one with ourselves and with those around us. Navajo mythology isn't sure about the eternal, but it is positive about the need to live at peace with one's self in this life. Every area of life must work in symmetry with every other area. Our walk must match our talk. Our words must be at one with our purpose. Only then is "hozho" possible.

Hopi theology talks about *koyaanisqatsi*, the state of being when one's life is out of balance. The Hopi are a very religious people. One of the goals of their faith is the avoidance of *koyaanisqatsi*. When one isn't right with one's family, the earth, or oneself, *koyaanisqatsi* is the result. Like the pocket watch with the broken staff, a person living in *koyaanisqatsi* no longer serves the purpose for which he or she was made.

The Greeks call it *eirene*, their word for peace. In Greek mythology, Eirene (our modern name Irene) was a daughter of Zeus and Themis. She was one god who loved to be involved in the affairs of humans. Together with her sisters, Eunomia (good order) and Dike (justice) she was thought to control human order and society. Collectively, they were known as the horae ("hours," interestingly enough). The Greeks believed that Eirene helped them be successful. In fact her baby daughter Ploutos is the goddess of wealth. Economic prosperity went hand-in-hand with peace.

In the human body, balance is a function connected to the ears. Metaphorically that is a potent image. To be at balance in one's life, one must learn to listen. To know peace, one must be able and willing to hear the voice of God. One must listen to one's friends, co-workers, spouse, and family members to learn from their collective wisdom. When one listens, one can also be an instrument of balance in the life of another. One who won't listen sings a solo. There is no harmony in a solo. Harmony comes from the Greek word for agreement. Harmony comes when two or more notes, thoughts, or purposes are in balance with each other.

I haven't had much balance in my life lately. Work has been very stressful. There are many demands on me. Many people depend on me. I feel the weight. It is very hard to relax. I have a lack of singleness of focus that makes harmony in my life impossible. When out of balance, the Native Americans of old would go into a lodge and burn the impurities out of their body through their sweat. They would take time apart to reflect, think, and clear their minds. Maybe that is what I need to do. Next week is a start. I am going to do my very best to take a week's vacation. I need to find some balance, some harmony, some eirene, and some hozho in my life. Like my injured Howard pocket watch, I feel like my balance is broken.

May God grant me the strength and the wisdom to once again serve the purpose for which I was made. Maybe you can't pronounce or fully understand the Hopi *koyaanisqatsi*, but each of you knows how important the balance is to the watch. My prayer is that you will each dedicate yourselves to finding peace, harmony, and balance in your life.

Amen and Amen

Standing the Test of Time

To a watch enthusiast, the term "the test of time" may refer to how many seconds variance from true time a given watch runs, or how long it takes for a watch to arrive after it has been ordered.

In a review of several websites, all the following are said to "stand the test of time:"

- Well-built buildings
- Poetry
- The Beatles
- Fine Wine
- Monopoly
- Gordie Howe

I don't know about those. I do know that there are certain attributes that go a long way towards enabling our lives to stand the test of time. I offer four to you for your consideration:

Decision-Making: Do your decisions stand the test of time? Are they carefully thought through? Father Theodore Hesburgh, president emeritus of The University of Notre Dame says: "My basic principle is that you don't make decisions because they are easy; you don't make them because they are cheap; you don't make them because they're popular; you make them because they're right." It takes courage to make right decisions. Once made, do you implement them, or allow them to lay dormant? When made, do you stick by them? Brian Tracy, personal effectiveness guru, states: "Your decision to be, have, and do something out of the ordinary entails facing difficulties that are out of the ordinary as well. Sometimes your greatest asset is simply your ability to stay with it longer than anyone else." Will the decisions you have made stand the test of time?

Faith: Does your faith stand the test of time? Faith is often the stuff that sustains us through turbulent times. Faith is the ability to vision the invisible, touch the untouchable, know the unknowable, and believe that which cannot, by the rationale mind alone, be believed. In Greek, faith and belief are so linked that they come from the same root word *pisteuo*. Those with strong faith have a knowledge others lack. In English, the term epistemology is the study of how we "know" things. The pragmatist misses out on the beauty of the invisible. The skeptic misses out on the caress of the untouchable.

I have always enjoyed the fact that the British have turned the word faith into a verb. They use the word faith as we use the word believe. They faith something they truly believe in. In what do you faith? Does your faith stand the test of time?

Hope: Do you have hope that stands the test of time? I think there is a difference between faith and hope. Hope is the obstinate endurance of belief in someone or something. We often use the term hope as a kind of conditional expectation. Hope is not a vain or vapid anticipation of something. It is much more rock solid than that. In reality it is a statement; a statement of belief prior to or contrary to known circumstances. We all too often cheapen hope. True hope carries a very high price and a very great risk.

In my professional singing career, I have performed the role of two of the kings in the Menotti opera *Amahl and the Night Visitors*. Amahl is the young shepherd boy who offers his crutch to the baby Jesus and is miraculously cured of his lameness. Amahl is an Arabic word for hope. The first step Amahl takes without his crutch is his step of hope. How about you? Do you take steps of hope? Do you have hope that stands the test of time?

Love: Does your love stand the test of time? I love spaghetti. I love watches. I love my wife. I love football. Love is one of the most overused and over-saturated words in the English language. Truly loving something or someone involves giving of yourself. I have yet to figure out how to give myself to a plate of spaghetti!

In the Greek language, there are three words for love, only one of which stands the test of time. The first, *eros*, is an earthy sensual love. We get our word erotic from it. The second, *phileo*, is a kind of brotherly or affiliative love. My name, Philip, uses that one (phileo-lover; hippo-horse). It literally means "lover of horses." The third, *agape* is the love that gives, the love that risks, and the love that hurts, the love that stands the test of time.

There is an interesting encounter in the New Testament between Jesus and Peter. Jesus asks Peter, "Do you love (*agape*) me?" Peter answers, "Lord, I love (*phileo*) you." Not the same thing, is it? Peter ultimately learns to love (*agape*) Jesus, follows him to his death, and is today venerated as the head of the Catholic Church.

Is there any *agape* kind of love in your life? Mother Teresa said: "We can do no great things; only small things with great love." Does your love stand the test of time?

Decision-making, faith, hope, and love...four attributes that help our lives stand the test of time. Will your life stand the ultimate horological test; the test of time?

Amen and Amen

How the Grandfather Clock Got its Name

Over 200 years ago in Piercebridge, North Yorkshire, England, there was a charming traveler's haven known as the George Hotel. The hotel was a routine stop for horse coaches and was managed by two bachelor brothers named Jenkins.

A floor clock, as they were called back in those days was the predominant feature of the lobby. It had been there for many years. One unusual characteristic of the old clock was that it kept very good time. This was uncommon, since in those days clocks were generally not noted for their accuracy. One day, one of the brothers died and suddenly the old clock started losing time. At first it lost 15 minutes per day. By the time several clockmakers gave up trying to repair the ailing timepiece, it was losing more than an hour each day.

The clock's incurable problem became as widely talked about as had its former precision. Some said it was no surprise that, though fully wound, the old clock stopped when the surviving brother died at the age of ninety. The new manager of the hotel never attempted to have it repaired. He just left it standing in a sunlit corner of the lobby, its hands resting in the position they assumed the moment the last Jenkins brother died.

About 1875, an American songwriter named Henry Work happened to be staying at the George Hotel during a trip to England. He was told the story of the old clock. After seeing the clock for himself, he decided to compose a song. The song focused on the fascinating coincidence that the clock stopped forever the moment its elder owner passed away. Upon returning to America, Henry published the lyrics and sold over a million copies of sheet music. These are the opening words of the first stanza:

My grandfather's clock was too tall for the shelf so it stood ninety years on the floor. It was taller by half than the old man himself, though it weighed not a pennyweight more. It was bought on the morn of the day that he was born, and was always his treasure and pride; But it stopped short- never to go again- when the old man died.

One Example of the Sheet Music (Photo in Public Domain)

According to the publishers of the song, it became the most popular song in America in the late nineteenth century. Until that time, clocks such as the one in the old George Hotel were referred to by a variety of names. Not before Henry Work wrote his song, over a hundred years ago, were they referred to as grandfather clocks.

Did you know there was a story behind how the grandfather clock got its name? Now you do. . . .

During the time I was in private practice in a pastoral counseling setting, I spent thousands of hours listening to people's stories. I became acutely aware that people's lives are not as simple as they often appear. Until you know someone's story you really don't know him or her at all.

Many of the stories I heard seemed like fictional novels. But, to the person recounting them, they were very real. Personal stories are like fingerprints. No two are the same. They are intrinsically bound up in the identity of the person, nay they are the identity of the person.

When a friend or a family member shares their story with you, they are sharing their most precious and private possession. Take time to listen. Put aside the mundane and enter into their hearts and lives. They will be enriched by telling you their story. You will be enriched by hearing it. Until you are aware of someone's life experiences: their pain, fears, and joys, you really don't know them at all. You cannot force someone to tell you his or her story. But when it is offered to you, stop everything and listen. They are giving you the most precious gift they have, the gift of self-revelation. Guard the story once you hear it. Honor their faith in you by honoring their confidence.

We all have a story. It is our most precious and most guarded possession. Your story began before you were born. Chapter on chapter have been written by you and by those who have touched your life for good or for ill. Please remember, it is rarely ever too late to write a new chapter or to revise an old one.

It isn't even the conclusion of your story when someone writes "The End" as death comes to you. You continue to influence other's stories by how you lived your life and how you touched those around you. Contrary to the old grandfather clock the hands of their lives don't stop when you pass away. Please leave them a heritage of hope and aspiration that they can take with them as they remember the role you played in their lives.

Amen and Amen

The story of the grandfather clock and the words to the song's sheet music were taken from:

http://www.theclockdepot.com/history_of_the_grandfather_clock.ht ml

And used with permission. Thanks, *The Clock Depot*!

The Sound of Silence

My wife and I are very different. I am a night-owl. I am writing this homily at 11:35 on Saturday night. I am wide awake and ready to write. My wife is dead asleep and has been for hours. She will be up wide awake at 5 a.m. ready to greet the day with joy and enthusiasm. My preferred body rhythm is to go to bed at 2 a.m. and get up at 10 a.m. The world, however, refuses to adapt to my rhythm. People expect me to meet them at 8 a.m. or even for breakfast at 7 a.m. This is not good unless there is scrapple!

No amount of coffee helps. I tried hunting once. They expected me to get up at 3:30 a.m. I never did that again. Tried fishing twice and had the same problem. Thanks to heavenly providence I am allergic to hay. I never could make it on a farm. The cows would burst before I ever got around to them. I don't believe I have ever seen a sunrise. I don't want to and don't need to. I have seen plenty of sunsets. It probably looks like the same thing just in the opposite direction!

Now you know my secret! The only watch or clock that I can't stand is an alarm clock. I never met an alarm clock that I liked. I hate wake-up calls at hotels, especially those computerized ones. Of course I also hate it when they don't call and I am late. I can't stand people who are cheerful in the morning. Quite frankly, I can't stand anybody in the morning. I like flying west! I get to stay up later and get up later. I love the joy of getting up at 6 a.m. realizing that it is really 9 a.m. Now that is my kind of trip!

Thinking about those awful creatures called alarm clocks I decided to conduct a Google search to find out what kind of evil lurks behind the minds of alarm clock makers. Here is what I found:

- **Zen Alarm Clocks:** They wake you up with a single gong that strikes once, reverberating for three minutes! Over ten minutes it works it way up to one strike every four seconds. Spare me!

- **Traffic Alarm Clocks:** They check the local traffic before they wake you up and announce the gridlock while waking you up. Why get up then?

- **Astronomical Alarm Clocks:** They tell you what constellations are in the sky in your exact location at the exact time you are being awakened! How useful can that be at 10am?

- **Desktop Dozen Alarm Clock:** They can be set to go off at five different times each day. Four more count-down alarms would be my worst nightmare! Why is called Dozen?

- **The Kisho Kurokawa Alarm Clock:** "Kisho Kurokawa is one of the foremost contemporary architects of Japan. Kurokawa's use of geometric figures is in keeping with his strong sense of balance in all his work. Kurokawa employs his concept of "abstract symbolism" throughout his work." Yep, that is just what I want; abstract symbolism at 5 a.m. in the morning!

- **Nature Sounds Alarm Clock:** Gives you your choice of more than twelve programmable natural sounds to soothingly wake you up. I prefer Simon and Garfunkel's hit classic *The Sound of Silence.*

- **The Shake Awake Vibrating Alarm Clock:** "Shake Awake is the world's new and innovative vibrating alarm clock. This incredible device is already making it easier for the 28 million Americans who experience some degree of hearing loss. Shake Awake is perfect for the 'morning impaired.'" Now I know what is wrong with me. I am "morning impaired." Hmm, wonder if I can go out on sick leave on that one. Then I could sleep in every morning. Hmm, I wonder where I put the quarter in this vibrating clock?

- **The Body Clock:** "Wake up gently as light fills the room with the Bodyclock™ dawn simulator that gives you your own personal sunrise!" Pleeze, that is the last thing I want!

Dr. Ronda Wimmer of Cal Poly Pomona explains it all to us this way:

> The use of biorhythms or circadian rhythms is categorized as chronobiology within the Western scientific community. Chronobiology is defined as "the study of rhythm patterns in biological phenomena." In Eastern philosophy, yin and yang aspects of the circadian clock represent an extremely important external synchronizer. This is based upon the transitional yin and yang rhythms of yin (nighttime/the sun going down) passing into yang (daytime/the sun coming up). These transitional rhythms are broken down into four quadrants within a 24-hour period. This clock gets even more specific, and also represents the times at which qi and blood are at their peak within each respective zang/fu organ. Each organ has a two-hour window that represents one organ entering the next, in a clockwise order of progression.

Well, now I understand for sure! Only in Southern California! I think my zang/fu organ needs some zang/fu Viagra!

Actually I am just a kid at heart, an adolescent who has never grown up. The USDA confirms this with their research: "Two Minneapolis-area school districts decided to shift secondary school start times to 8:30 a.m. or later, based on emerging medical research showing adolescents have a natural sleep pattern that leads to a late-to-bed, late-to-rise cycle."

Well, now you know the rest of the story. Phather Phil is morning impaired and is still an adolescent in mind and body (my wife would confirm that). It is now 1:09 a.m. and I am raring to go. The dogs are asleep. My son is asleep. My wife is asleep. I call for the Night Owls of America to unite to free us all from the bondage and tyranny of alarm clocks. Are you with me?

Oh well, God has made us all different. Some of us just have enough sense to avoid early morning traffic jams! Oh no, here is a note I just found from my wife. She wants to go to the early church service! Yikes!

Amen and Amen

The Gain in the Loss

As much as we all love time and keeping time, there are some things in life for which there is never a good time. From my own personal experience here are a few:

- For an eleven-year old girl to be abducted and killed.
- To have your dad go into the hospital for a knee operation and have him never come home; dying of cancer in the same hospital within weeks. We didn't even know he was sick.
- To try for months to adopt a disabled child, only to find out the doctors have declared him unadoptable.
- To walk in a room in a mud hut to discover a cobra coiled and staring at you just three feet away.
- To buy a beautiful watch and drop it within ten minutes, breaking it.
- To fail to be awarded a major contract by .32 of one point.
- To be told you have Lou Gehrig's disease.
- To make a big deal about things that don't really matter.
- To lose your temper and hurt those you love.
- To have a friend call you from all the way across the country for a shoulder to lean on and not know what to say to make it better.

While there is never a good time for any of these things, there is good that can come out of experiencing them. In the same order:

- Watching a community come together in tremendous support, prayer, and caring for a devastated family.
- Getting closer to a dad who was always distant.
- The joys of watching the child improve; causing the doctors to change their minds.

- The strength that comes from learning you can handle adverse, even dangerous situations.
- Having a watchmaker friend pick it up off the floor, assuring you he can fix it better than ever.
- Trying again and knowing the rush of winning the contract by thirty points.
- The joys of having the doctor call later that week, saying he was wrong.
- This is the hardest one of all. Maturity and wisdom come from learning the difference between the things that matter and those that don't.
- To know the increased intimacy and fun that comes from working it out.
- Another tough one; to be honored for being asked and to be humbled for not having the answers.

At different times, life brings us hurt, pain, shame, fear, and loss. It is often those very same times when we learn the most about ourselves. It is often those very same times when we learn the most period. Let us not dread the losses. Let us have the patience and perseverance to experience the gain God has for us in the loss. Like the blacksmith's forge of old, life's pains are often the fire through which we must go to be made strong.

When the watch is wound, tension is applied. As time goes on that tension is released, producing the smooth flow and functioning of all of the watch's parts. So it is with life.

Amen and Amen

A Time for Peace

War is a terrible thing. Sometimes it makes for strange coincidences. Whoever would have thought the young Rebel at Shiloh and the young Yankee in confederate prison in North Carolina would have so much in common?

Young Hank S. was a raw Rebel recruit from Arkansas. He had never seen combat before that April 6th in 1862. More Americans would die in the two days of the battle of Shiloh than in all the Revolutionary War, War of 1812, and Mexican War combined. Recalling his first glimpse of the Yankees, the young Rebel later wrote in his diary, "I at last saw a row of little globes of smoke streaked with crimson, breaking out with spurtive quickness from a long line of bluey figures in front; and, simultaneously, there broke upon our ears an appalling crash of sound."

The young teenager, Bobby L. had run away from home. He kept on running all the way from Scotland to America. He had dropped out of school and had run to America in search of adventure. The civil war broke out and Bobby enlisted in the Union Army under a false name, so as not to embarrass his family back in Scotland. He did not think his father would approve. From Virginia, Bobby wrote his dad, "To bear your name here would lead to further dishonoring it. I have never hurt anyone knowingly in battle, having always fired high." The Rebels, however, were not so kind. Bobby soon found himself a prisoner at the Confederate prison in Salisbury, North Carolina. Young Hank S. survived Shiloh and the war. Young Bobby L. was killed by his guards during a mass break-out attempt at Salisbury.

Their connection? Bobby L's full and real name was Robert Livingstone. He was the son of David Livingstone the famous Scottish medical missionary and explorer in Africa.

Hank S was Henry Stanley. Henry survived the war, went on to become a renowned newspaper reporter and in an encounter immortalized by history, "found" Dr. David Livingstone, Robert's father, in the heart of Africa. This once young rebel was the man of "Dr. Livingstone, I presume?" fame.

Hank and Bobby never met. They served on different sides of America's most terrible tragedy. Their lives were forever linked together in the person of Dr. David Livingstone.

Ecclesiastes 3 tells us there is a "time for war" and a "time for peace." It goes on to state there is a "time to kill" and a "time to heal." I am not sure what time it is right now.

We are engaged in a war right now with great potential to unite and to divide. It is my prayer that the time for war and for killing will be quickly over. It is my prayer that the time for peace and for healing will be long lasting and enduring.

Let us all pray for the safety of our troops and of the people of Iraq, together with the security of the entire Middle East. May God quickly bring us through the time of war to the time of peace.

Amen and Amen

Simple and True Truth

In his famous "Essay on Criticism," Alexander Pope made the following observation:

"Tis with our Judgments as our Watches, none go just alike, yet each believes his own."

Today I received in the mail a beautiful watch. It is well-made and nicely decorated. It is a beautiful thing to behold. Upon opening the certificate that came with the watch, I observed the results of five tests of the watch in five basic positions. The watch had different degrees of variance from true time depending on the position it was in; yet in every position it varied just a little.

I was struck by the similarity of that watch to my own life. Integrity is important to me, yet I often find myself varying from simple and true truth depending on the position I am in. Were my comments and thoughts to be measured against true truth, I wonder if I would pass the test and be considered a reliable indicator of what is true?

So it is, as Mr. Pope said, with my judgments. I have strong beliefs. I argue well. Take me on in a war of words at your own peril. May God give me the grace to realize that I am not always right. I must understand my view of the world may not always represent the truth of how it is. May I have enough peace of mind and heart to recognize when in one position or another, I often fail the test.

Wade Davis, a well-known anthropologist said it well, "The world in which you were born is just one model of reality. Other cultures are not failed attempts at being you. They are unique manifestations of the human spirit."

Just as my new watch does not perfectly tell time; neither am I always right in my judgments or beliefs. I want to be a certified chronometer in life. May God help me to pass the test regardless of my situation or position.

Amen and Amen

The Blisters of Life

As of late, I haven't liked Phather Phil (my name on the watch boards) very much. I have been stressed by many things; have been irritable, and generally not very nice. I have let things get to me, not always big things just irritating things. Two events have happened recently that have caught my attention.

I love to work in the yard. I recently cleaned out a back corner of our yard and planted an orange tree. I used white cement edging to finish off the bed. I bought a bunch, but found myself five short to finish the job. I went to Home Depot, got a push cart and loaded them on. Just as I was finishing, a Home Depot employee came up to me and announced that all the scalloped white edging was sold, including that which I had just placed on my cart. He told me I would have to come back on Tuesday when they would have more. He reached down and began pulling my edging (emphasis on "my") off my cart and back on their pallet. It was hot, I wanted to get the job done and had just loaded my cart. His act violated my space, my work, and just plain made me mad. If they were all sold, why was there no sign so indicating? I let him have it. My wife says my verbal skills are legendary, especially when I am mad. I reamed him out royally using my best homiletic skills. I was angry, loud, and inappropriate. I gained little satisfaction from my tirade. I was especially unhappy when I turned around to see one of my former students standing there staring at me in shock. I am a spiritual leader and mentor to him and his family. I was embarrassed. I don't think the Home Depot guy should have removed the edging out of my cart as he did, but that did not excuse my tirade.

The very next day the beautiful Jamo speakers that I bought for our home stereo system arrived. Setting them up properly involved moving the back surround sound speakers. That involved running new wires through our attic to the back wall of the living room. I started that task about 2:00 p.m. in the afternoon on a very hot sunny Sarasota day. The attic was like a furnace. My wife added to the fiery furnace by suggesting I should have done it at 7:00 a.m. when it was still cool. She has been married to me for thirty-three years. She knows I don't do anything at 7:00 a.m. If the rapture occurs at 7:00 a.m., I will probably sleep through it!

I only needed to change one more wire. Sure enough, after crawling through insulation, trying not to crash through the drywall ceiling, and tripping over the air conditioning ducts, I discovered that I had pulled the wrong wire. I had pulled the wire that didn't need changed. Now I had to replace that one and still pull the new one. I took the new one, drilled a hole, put the wire down through it, and told my wife to hang on to the wire. I went back across the attic to find the good wire that I had wrongly pulled. Just as I got there, she let go of the wire she was supposed to hold to, and of course, it sprang back through the hole like a spring. A half hour in Florida afternoon hades and nothing accomplished!

I threw a fit up there in that attic. I cursed; something that rarely happens. Of course I felt no better after my fit and the wires were still not where they should be. Worse yet I so upset my son by my fit that he cursed at me. That stopped me dead in my tracks. My son is twenty-five years old. I have never heard him curse. I realized he was parroting me. That really upset me.

Did I mention the snake? While sweating it out in the attic, I heard a terrible commotion in the garage. While helping me, my wife discovered a baby brown water snake coiled up in the corner. Oh the joys of living in Florida. She took a trowel to it and that ended the life of one brown snake! During all that excitement I was stuck up in attic hell.

I came down out of the attic shaking with heat, frustration, and sadness. I apologized to all, but didn't feel any better. I had a big glass of iced tea, wrapped a cold wet towel around my neck, and went back up to hades. All went well and in no time beautiful surround sound was emanating from all the speakers. They are hung with care and the sound is terrific.

Two events in two days shamed ole Phather Phil. I decided it was time for a change. I decided it was time to step back, relax, and stop letting irritations get to me. I was changing in a way I didn't like. I decided to make every effort to get control of my emotions, will, and tongue. It was time to change.

Then, a few days later I read an article in the local paper in Apalachicola, FL. It was about a fellow who bought a new pair of shoes. The next morning he put them on to go to work. By the time he got to work, he discovered that they were too tight and had caused quite a big blister to develop. He was angry about the shoes and the blister. He grudgingly decided he needed to take the time to go to a drugstore and buy some Band-Aids. Doing all that made him twenty minutes late for work. That day was Sept 11, 2001 and he worked in one of the Trade Towers in New York City. The blister had saved his life. I am not sure if that story is true or an urban myth. But, it sure spoke to me. It suggested to me that I need not be angry at the irritating things that come my way. Irritations, the blisters of life, are not always bad.

How about you? How have you been handling irritations, disappointments, and frustrations lately? Phather Phil has had to face himself and come to the realization that it is time to take a time out. I am fifty-four years of age and still need to grow and learn better how to control my reactions. I pray that each of you will have the strength and wisdom to know when to take time out to reassess your life, to chill out (even when in attic hades) and to be patient with all that life throws at you. I wish you each the courage to know when it is time to take time, when it is time to change, and when it is time to truly count your blessings; in spite of life's many frustrations.

Amen and Amen

Sometimes it's the Small Things

There are many important passages in life. Many time periods in one's life are formative. I personally believe that one of the most important is that time between 22 and 26 years of age. Adult patterns and behaviors are set during that time. Worldviews are concretized; beliefs are adjusted and confirmed, or cast away.

During that time in my life, I was blessed with a wonderful mentor and coach. In the late sixties and early seventies there were no Dr. Ruth's. Dr. Phil was probably off somewhere in college or high school. Popular psychology was unpopular. The APA frowned on it, sponsored papers against it, and disciplined its members for offering advice in anything but the intimacy of the counseling suite.

Against that backdrop, a licensed psychologist arose in Southern California who had tremendous appeal to a huge group of people. Dr. Clyde Narramore was the first popularizer of psychology/counseling to the masses. The fact that he did this predominately in a religiously based culture made his impact even more remarkable. Dr. Narramore was on hundreds of radio stations, wrote over 100 books and had newspaper columns in papers all across the country. "Psychology for Living" was his moniker. He traveled the world preaching and teaching a mixture of pop psychology and theology that was mixed with a wonderfully warm and genuine sense of personal attention. He was gracious, self-confident and brilliant. For several years, I was his personal assistant.

I was none of those things. I was barely post adolescent, full of doubts and internal uncertainties even though I had always been one of the best at anything I did. Because of that I was always placed in groupings that included the best. The problem is that I was always one of the worst of the best. No matter how well I did things, I was always the worst of the group. I ran track . . . made the track team but was the slowest on the team. I made a select group of oratorio singers, but was the worst singer of the 24. I made the academic quiz team from my university, but was the dumbest on the team and so on . . .

Dr. Narramore changed a lot for me. I was his personal assistant. He taught me to write. He was the best writer I have ever met. He taught me to believe in myself.

He believed in himself more than any other individual I had ever met. The APA haunted him. The religious community rejected him for interposing psychology with theology. Yet he single-mindedly moved on . . . unwaveringly committed to helping people. He taught me and encouraged me in so many ways. He went off to Europe to speak and would let me keep pumping out his newspaper columns. He had unwavering faith in me. That faith has never left me.

He taught me I could dare to dream to do great things . . . big things . . . important things.

In retrospect, in my own mind I have attained very little of that. I still however, have that belief that someday I might just achieve. Every day when I sit at the computer working on my book, *River's Mourning Song*, I think maybe it will be my achievement . . . my "great" thing that I will leave behind me.

I have three things on my desk: a wonderful quote on writing by Stephen King, a picture of my wife, and one of Dr. Narramore's books. They work together to keep me writing . . . believing . . . daring.

This spring has been an uncertain time for me. My health has been up and down and up and down. My work has been up and down. My self-confidence has been mostly down. My energy has been down. My aspirations have faded a bit against the glare of life.

However, sometimes it's the small things.

Two days ago I arrived home from Fort Lauderdale. Waiting for me was a new Zenith watch. It is a rare, kinky, funny, unique kind-of-a-watch. It defies description. It is the color of *Beer and Brat Mustard* (my favorite brand). It has the same spice as that mustard. It is elegant. It is funky. It is all things and nothing anyone could want in a watch. The bracelet was too big for my wrist. I started sizing it down to fit me. I immediately knew that was to be no easy task. Zenith bracelets are sturdy and beautiful. They are not meant for the layman to size. Sleeves and pins stubbornly resist the amateur's touch. There are no finite adjustments . . . it is link or lose!

Since confronted by my illness and discouragements this spring I have begun to focus on the small things. Paying more attention to the "every day" has become far more important to me. Being pain-free for an hour, then a day, and so on was important.

Back to the bracelet . . . I dared . . . it defied. I renewed my efforts. It resisted with an equal fervor. I removed one pin only to be confronted by a sleeve. On and on it went. My wife began to get that worried look on her face. You know . . . the one that says "Honey, just take it to Mr. K tomorrow, he can do it!" Mr. K is a wonderful European watchmaker here in Sarasota. He can do anything horological. Two nights ago it was important that I do it. Taking it to Mr. K would have signaled defeat in a small thing.

I persevered in my offense. The bracelet remained resolute in its defense. I maneuvered. It mocked. I got out my hammer. My wife panicked. The watch stared at me with a harsh unfearful kind of yellow contempt. I persevered. I sized. It gave way, but didn't fit. I tried one more half-link then another. I tentatively placed it on my wrist. It fit! It didn't just fit. It fit wonderfully well. I had achieved a big victory in a small thing.

Nothing great happened that evening. Nothing memorable emanated from our living room. However, I had persevered. I achieved. I smiled a big smile.

Putting my tools back in my watch bag, I felt that I had just written the great American novel. The Pulitzer Prize was mine. I wore my Zenith all day yesterday with a sense of pride. It is a beautiful watch.

More importantly, it represented a big victory in a small thing. Those are the things that fill life; the things we dare not ignore on our journey to feeling good about ourselves. My encouragement to each of you . . . Grab hold of one small victory today. Make it your own. Don't miss out on it on your life's journey. Hold on to one thing that makes you smile.

Remember; sometimes it's the small things.

Amen and Amen

A Time for Us

Wouldn't it be great if there were a positive correlation between the number of watches you own and the amount of time you have? Unfortunately, at least for me, it doesn't work that way.

When I was in college (1967-71) I needed financial help to make it through. I received a half scholarship for academics and a half scholarship for singing bass in the college public relations team. We sang in churches and high schools all over the Midwest, recruiting students and telling the story of the school.

That was the sixties and the most popular songs we sang were "The Age of Aquarius" and "A Time for Us" (the theme song from the hit movie "Romeo and Juliet). For those of you who are much too young to know this song, the words go something like this:

A time for us, some day there'll be
When chains are torn by courage born of a love that's free
A time when dreams so long denied can flourish
As we unveil the love we now must hide

A time for us, at last to see
A life worthwhile for you and me

And with our love, through tears and thorns
We will endure as we pass surely through every storm
A time for us, some day there'll be a new world
A world of shining hope for you and me

Lyrics by Andy Williams © Sony/ATV Music Publishing LLC

I met my wife in freshman English in 1968. We have now been married thirty-one years. Through all the early years of graduate school, ministry, and teaching, we kept thinking that someday there would be "A Time for Us." We worked, we studied, and we ministered, knowing that someday there would be "A Time for Us."

In the early eighties I was so busy writing, teaching, counseling, and ministering that I almost lost the "Us." I came very close to blowing it. I came very close to losing my wife for the sake of all I was doing. "A Time for Us" very nearly never came.

This week, my hope for all you watchaholics is that in addition to your fascination with watchmakers that you will become time makers; that you will force yourselves by an act of your will to make time. Make time for those people who really matter in your life. To those of you who spend hours *timing your watches, make sure you also watch your timing.*

I would guess most of you are in your late twenties or early thirties. You still have time, in the words of the song, to make "a life worthwhile." Take it from someone who has owned many watches, but wasted much time, there is nothing like taking ownership of "a world of shining hope" for you and those important to you. Put your lives under the same scrutiny you put your watches. Make time.

Yesterday our family had a good time. We rested and relaxed together. Last night we had a good time attending a local concert by our favorite singing group *Rockapella*. Wow, can those guys sing!

I wore a watch all day yesterday, not to tell time, but to remind me to make time - "A Time for Us."

Unfortunately, there is no correlation between having more watches and having more time. Therefore, my homily today is to encourage each of you to make time for those who you love. Don't wait for someday. Do it today.

Amen and Amen

Perseverance Makes the Hero

Heroes . . . At different times in my life I have had different heroes. The earliest one I remember was Davy Crockett. The fifties were filled with Davy Crockett, king of the wild frontier. My fake coonskin hat was my prized possession.

As I got older I moved on to Mickey Mantle. He was every baseball player's hero in the late fifties and early sixties. Yet, he drank excessively and had too many home runs off the field. Neil Armstrong and John Wayne were big heroes. Joe Frazier, from Philadelphia, ranked up there for me. Billy Graham was a hero. An old man now, he is untouched by scandal . . . what a relief.

As time passed and I aged, my heroes changed. As I matured, my heroes became great writer/theologians like C.S. Lewis and Charles Haddon Spurgeon. My favorite of all was David Livingstone. Now there was a hero. Born among Scotland's poor . . . buried among Westminster Abbey's great. Please go rent "David Livingstone" starring Spencer Tracy . . . there never has been a better movie.

Time moves on. Now, at fifty-four years of age, I look for even greater heroes. It is much harder today for someone to reach hero level than when I was ten. Time has a way of increasing standards. Today I have one hero. That hero is my business partner. He is my hero because he is everything I would like to be. He is strong, faithful, loyal, and untiringly loving to his wife.

You see, Frank's wife has a rare brain disease. Ever since I have known him (early 1997), she has been sick . . . bed-ridden . . . invalid. Frank is faithful and loyal to her in every way. That was tested this past week. She was very sick . . . almost died several times. Lots of stress for all of us, yet Frank persevered. He is a model of loyalty, love, and faithfulness. For that, I am grateful. For that, he is my hero.

Frank is able to love his wife while seeking and getting nothing in return. That kind of love is a rare commodity in these times. He has never given up. He has never given out.

Florence Nightingale said: "I am of certain convinced that the greatest heroes are those who do their duty in the daily grind of domestic affairs whilst the world whirls as a maddening dreidel." Given that definition, Frank is the greatest hero I know.

What has this to do with time? I answer that with one word . . . perseverance. Being faithful, being a hero involves hanging in there over time. Many are those who are strong for a moment. Heroes persevere over time.

May God grant us each the fortitude to be heroes, remaining true in our daily tasks through all that life throws at us. I am thankful for Frank. After all these years chasing coonskin caps, he has finally shown me what courage is all about.

Amen and Amen

The Big Rocks

The members of this forum spend a lot of time focusing on time. You would think that time management would be second nature to us. There is one particular story about time management that I really enjoy. No one knows who the author is or when it was first told. There are many different versions. It always challenges me when I hear it or tell it:

One day, an expert in time management was speaking to a group of business students and, to drive home a point, used an illustration those students will never forget. As he stood in front of the group of high-powered overachievers he said, "Okay, time for a quiz" and he pulled out a one-gallon wide-mouth mason jar and set it on the table in front of him. He also produced about a dozen fist-sized rocks and carefully placed them, one at a time, into the jar.

When the jar was filled to the top and no more rocks would fit inside, he asked, "Is this jar full?" Everyone in the class yelled, "Yes." The time management expert replied, "Really?" He reached under the table and pulled out a bucket of gravel. He dumped some gravel in and shook the jar causing pieces of gravel to work themselves down into the spaces between the big rocks.

He then asked the group once more, "Is the jar full?" By this time the class was on to him. "Probably not," one of them answered "Good!" he replied. He reached under the table and brought out a bucket of sand. He started dumping the sand in the jar and it went into all of the spaces left between the rocks and the gravel.

Once more he asked the question, "Is this jar full?" "No!" the class shouted. Once again he said, "Good." Then he grabbed a pitcher of water and began to pour it in until the jar was filled to the brim. Then he looked at the class and asked, "What is the point of this illustration?"

One eager beaver raised his hand and said, "The point is, no matter how full your schedule is, if you try really hard you can always fit some more things in it!" "No," the speaker replied, "That's not the point. The truth this illustration teaches us is: If you don't put the big rocks in first, you'll never get them in at all."

What are the 'big rocks' in your life: Your faith, time with your loved ones, a worthy cause, teaching or mentoring others, your education, or your dreams? Remember to put these BIG ROCKS in first or you'll never get them in at all. So, tonight, or in the morning, when you are reflecting on this short story, ask yourself this question: What are the *big rocks* in my life? Then, put those in your jar first.

Amen and Amen

River's Mourning Song

It was nineteenth century Florida at its best. Dirt roads meandered through hammocks of cabbage palms and water oaks. Spanish moss, some fifteen to twenty feet in length hung like angel's hair from hidden branches of mighty oaks. Gators, deer, wild turkeys, bobcat, and yes, even the occasional panther prowled the night. Deer had no fear of humans because there were lots of the former and few of the latter. The horizon went on forever. The sunset was God's way of bragging, showing off every beautiful color He had ever made.

Through the midst of it all, the river meandered like a silver serpent. It turned and twisted, playing "now you see me, now you don't." The bronzed canoeist could easily spot twenty to thirty gators sunning on its banks, wild hogs drinking their fill from its bounty, their eyes kept constantly on the big turtles that peered up from beneath the water like the silent periscopes of the deep.

The river wasn't terribly wide, maybe twenty-four feet at its widest point. The Calusa lived off of it for centuries. Trails to their winter fishing and hunting camps could clearly be seen. It was everything you vision when you close your eyes and think of the river of grass. It was the Everglades at their most primitive and at their finest.

Yet, it wasn't the nineteenth century. It was the last decade of the twentieth. Twelve acres of the palmed paradise and three-hundred feet of the river's banks were all ours.

It started out innocently enough . . . a small ad in the paper. A bankrupt restaurant destroyed a young family's dream. They had just built a home on twelve acres of vintage Florida wilderness. Now they had to sell. They had to sell quickly. My wife, son, and I went to see it. It was the second time in my life I experienced love at first sight (the other was in freshman English in college; that is a different story!). Within weeks the deed was done (literally).

My grasp of the English language is not adequate to tell you how much I loved that place. I knew every massive oak, the thousands of vines that wound their way through the woods and every trail down to the river. I once put out a lightning-caused Spanish moss fire with my bare hands (well, not quite with my bare hands). We spent hours, days, weeks, and months trying to keep the Everglades from taking the property back. Everything grew so fast . . . so very fast. Nothing was ever greener, quieter, or more romantic than those twelve acres.

Of course, nothing ever needed more mowing either. The drive into town for work was huge. The maintenance was constant. The expertise needed to keep it all up was sorely lacking in my seminary education. It was a place for rich folks to live. It was a place for the owner to enjoy . . . a plantation like setting where others were paid to do the work. We weren't rich.

So we decided to move back into Sarasota. It almost did me in. My head knew it was the right thing to do. My heart felt a pull similar to that when I would attach the tractor to a big old vine to yank it out of the trees. Leaving Hidden River was a big yank.

Through a mutual friend, we met a man who owned a little house within a mile of my wife's school. He kept it as rental property. He wanted a big house out in the country. We swapped houses! We signed so many papers that day! The deed was done again (literally). We gently closed the gate, peered over our shoulders with a sigh, and once again became city-dwellers.

I really didn't want to leave Hidden River. I wanted my company to grow faster so I could afford everything I needed to maintain twelve acres of paradise. It didn't. Moving back was the right thing to do.

Not all of life's decisions are pleasant. Some are just plain necessary. This one was necessary.

We moved back into Sarasota in 1999. It takes me fifteen minutes to mow my little yard. Hey, after all the rains last week, we even found a turtle in our yard and a snake in our garage . . . the sweet memories of Hidden River.

On Tuesday, June 24, 2003, less than two weeks ago, I was sitting in the Jackson, MS airport waiting a plane to take me home from a speaking engagement there. Bored, I was browsing through *USA Today*. Startled out of my airport-induced lethargy, I was stunned to read a small article in Section A. Apparently in a small river-front development in Florida's eastern Sarasota County, a levee had given way, causing severe damage as the river rampaged to forty of the ninety or so homes.

That's it . . . no name of the river, the development . . . nothing else. Never has my cell phone sprung into such sudden action. My wife knew nothing about it. She simply said it was still pouring and that the neighborhood kids were boogie-boarding down the middle of our street. She promised to turn the TV on and call me if she heard anything.

Ten minutes later she called me back. With a quivering voice, she told me that it was indeed Hidden River. My stomach flew into my throat. I felt nauseous and dizzy. Our tranquil Myakka River had become a raging demon, breaking through the levee, rushing the half-mile through the woods, flooding everything in its path. Our old house was in its path. The river didn't stop at the house; it continued through it, across the two acres in front, over the road and on to our neighbor's cattle pasture. Five to six feet of river rose in our old home.

Everything was destroyed.

The past two weeks I have repeatedly trembled at the thought of it all. The levee broke at 9:00AM Monday morning. I can't imagine the torrent of water. I can close my eyes to imagine it and nothing comes. My mind won't let me see it.

I buried our two pet dogs back in those woods. I sure hope they are ok. Isn't that a crazy thought? I am so worried about those dogs. I so lovingly placed them in that big hole I dug. I am so mad at that river for disturbing them.

Of course, the human toll is tremendous. Our hearts go out to all our old neighbors and friends. The police won't let us in now. The roads and houses are still flooded. I wonder if all the deer made it safely. Can wild turkeys fly? What about our neighbor's goats? What about my old dogs?

What do we do with all this?

The temptation is to be grateful and thank God that we don't live there anymore. The prideful spiritual mind says "God spared us by putting the urge in our minds to move. He honored our faith and trust in Him by sparing us from this terrible tragedy." That is what one-half of my mind says.

The other half rejects that and rebukes me for thinking that way. What about all the other people who still live there? Why wouldn't God have made them move? Our neighbors were all wonderful Godly people. They have now lost everything. They were not spared the crushing heartbreak of the river's rampage. Why were we? The simple answer is, we will never know.

The only thing that separates us from last week's Myakka River disaster is time. Three years ago we decided to move. Three years of time is our levee. No chronograph can measure three years of time. No sundial is that big. What I have learned through all this is that I need to have more faith and patience when I am faced with a decision that I don't particularly want to make. I have learned that I don't always have to understand everything. I have learned that what I may decry at the moment may very well turn out to be the best.

There is a greater irony.

I am writing a historical novel. Six months ago, I tentatively titled it, *River's Mourning Song*. The families in my novel participate in one tragedy after another, over one hundred-fifty years of time and two continents—all of them taking place in or on the banks of rivers. Rivers seem to me to be one of the greatest metaphors for life. But for the span of three years of time, I might have added my own personal chapter to *River's Mourning Song*.

Please join me in praying for the victims of Sarasota County's Myakka River disaster. They are good people. They were wonderful neighbors. My heart goes out to them all.

Amen and Amen

When Watches Tell More than Time

Sometimes watches do more than tell time. Sometimes they teach us lessons. Here are some watches and the lessons they have recently taught me:

1. Jacques Etoile Carbon LeMans Watch

I posted about this watch yesterday because it really bugged me. This watch has written "Swiss Made" on the front and "Made in Germany" on the back. After some reflection and some guidance from Steve of the Limes Watch Company, I think this watch is an anomaly. Better said, I think it is a mistake. I don't think Klaus Jakobs intended for the watch to say both.

Acknowledging that to be the case, it still has given me pause to reflect on whether or not I am a different person at different times, or in front of different people. I should be who and what I am consistently to all. The pressures to conform to my environment are great. May God give me the grace and strength to be content and consistent with whom I am.

2. Grand Seiko Watch

I have often "turned my nose up" at Seikos. No way I would ever buy or wear a Seiko. This Grand Seiko has taught me how foolish I have been. This is an incredibly beautiful watch. I should never have been so arrogant about Seikos. This watch has taught me that when my own biases limit me, I am the loser. I wonder how many other beautiful things and people I have missed out on with such an attitude?

3. Minerva Nostalgia Watch

I was sure there are two different versions of the Nostalgia. I was wrong. The two very different scans were the same watch! Apparently the dial has a silver mirror finish that reflects whatever color light hits it. It makes the same watch look very different.

I learned two things from this watch. First, I can be wrong. Wow, there I said it! Second, things are not always as they seem. I must often temper the strength and vehemence of my perceptions. I am not always right in my judgments. I must hesitate in life just enough to take a second look to make sure. This watch teaches me that when I'm sure that I am right I may be surely wrong.

4. Schwarz Etienne Flight Controller Watch

Perhaps this lesson is my favorite. I have been curious about the Flight Controller for a long time. When I saw one at an extremely reasonable price on the Internet I jumped at it. I didn't ask too many questions, just made an offer, and bought it. When it arrived I was very happy. In fact I am wearing it as I type this. It is the only watch I have worn since I got it! I am very pleased with it. Beautiful, big and bold!

I posted scans of the watch online because I was so happy and proud of it. Then it happened. I received an email from someone telling me that he was happy to see his old watch (identified by the number 81 engraved on the side). He said he had really liked it and regretted selling it. I wrote him back and thanked him for his message. I also asked him to tell me a little more about the history of the watch. He emailed me back and told me that he had bought it second hand from a dealer in Bangkok. He then told me he sold it to a buyer in Texas. I bought it from a seller in California. That made me (if I can still count) the fifth owner of the watch.

Now had I known that there were four previous owners of this watch, I probably would not have bought it. I would have assumed it would have been beat up or had something seriously wrong with it. My assumptions would have led me to miss out on what has become my favorite watch (at least in terms of wear time). I have learned from this watch that I must be open to all opportunities. When I make unfounded assumptions, I am only limiting myself. I pray that I don't miss my own next great adventure because of some misplaced preconception.

Yes, my watches tell me the time. Sometimes they also teach me really good lessons.

Amen and Amen

Setting our Clocks to Our Own Time

It is said that in the early fifties, a wonderful old gentleman owned a wonderful old clock shoppe. He sold wonderful watches and clocks. It was said he could fix any watch or clock that was ever made. He even had a bowl of mints on his counter for the wonderful children of every clock-loving parent in his wonderful small town.

He kept his very best clocks in the window of his store. He enjoyed people coming by to look at them. Sometimes they even came in to buy a particularly nice example. With a sigh, he would watch it leave his store. He was sad to see it go, yet happy it found a good home.

Every day about 8:30 am, just as he was opening his store a well-dressed gentleman would come by. Every morning the well-dressed gentleman stopped, pulled out his pocket watch, and set it by the beautiful big mantle clock that was the pride of the window display. The well-dressed gentleman never came in the store and never spoke a word. Every morning he stopped by and every morning he set his pocket watch. Every morning he smiled at the wonderful old clock shoppe man and every morning he went on his way.

After several months of this, the clock shoppe owner became curious as to who the well-dressed gentleman was. One day on purpose he was outside at 8:30 a.m. when the well-dressed gentleman came by. They smiled and greeted each other. After exchanging pleasantries, the well-dressed gentleman said, "I love that old mantle clock in the window, it is quite beautiful. Is it an accurate timekeeper?" Beaming with pride, the old clock shoppe man replied, "Oh yes, it keeps perfect time. I set it at noon every day by the big whistle from the factory just across the street. I then set all my other clocks by it. The next day it is right on time when the whistle blows again."

The well-dressed gentleman looked startled at this information; startled and puzzled. He softly said "I stop by here every morning and set my pocket watch by that mantle clock. Then, every day, when my pocket watch says it is noon I pull the factory whistle! You see, I am the owner of the factory just across the street."

The two men looked at each other with amazement as the reality of the truth of the matter sunk in. Indeed the whole town set their clocks by that factory whistle, which was set to the pocket watch, which was set to the mantle clock, which was set to the factory whistle!

There were no atomic clocks available to the public in the early fifties. It was hard to find a true standard against which to know the true time. Indeed, the residents of this small town, depending on that ever-popular whistle, were caught in a circle of time.

In so many ways, this story reminds me of popular culture today. We protest the existence of universal standards. We each set our values clock by the time that seems right to us. Sometimes we even brag about that, as if having various standards, is somehow, a virtue. Like the people of that small town we are depending on a circular popular standard to tell us what time it is. We may even assert that our values are set to the current popular thinking (the whistle), not realizing that the whistle is at best, set to itself! It is a norm without a standard.

Perhaps and just maybe, it is time to submit ourselves to those standards that have stood the test of time for centuries. Maybe it is time to evaluate how we live our lives against something that transcends our ever-changing concepts of what time it is. Our corporate world, our churches, our families, even our own individual lives seem at times to be so chaotic and standard-less.

Think how chaotic the world would be if every individual set his watch to his own time. Maybe, just maybe it is time for each of us to stop setting our clocks to our own time.

(The story of the clock shoppe and the factory has several different versions and the original author is unknown)

Amen and Amen

Hitting the Bulls-Eye

The Greek language has two basic words for time. The first and most common is chronos from which we get a variety of English words: chronometer, chronology, chronic, crony (did you know that one?), etc. It pretty literally means "time" as we know it. What perhaps you didn't know is that Saturn was an important Roman God. He ate five of his six children to keep them from usurping his throne. His sixth child, Jupiter survived and banished Saturn. Saturn then went to Rome and taught the Romans farming, an activity that has a strong time (seasonal) component. Saturn was a Roman God. His Greek counterpart was Chronos or Kronos. The representation of Saturn or Kronos was often a snake eating his own tail. In this mythological interpretation, time was seen as creating (giving birth) and then destroying that which it created (as did Kronos). Perhaps time does that in one way or another to all of us. Time marches forward causing the eventual entropy of all that it created. Things do change over time.

For example, I really like these old Canadian Oyster Watches. They are smallish, made mostly by Rolex/Tudor. One of my favorite Canadian Oyster watches is the *Solar Aqua King-of-Wings* (don't you love that name?) watch made by Rolex and Tudor for the Eaton's Department Store chain. At one time Eaton's ruled the retail world of Canada. Established in the late 1800's, by WWII it dominated Canadian retail sales. It was so big it had its own line of Rolex made watches. They called their watches the Solar line. Their most popular model was the *King-of Wings* 34 mm oyster cased watch.

By 1970, Eaton's was in trouble. By 1997 they were bought by Sears. Today, replaced by Sears, they are all closed or being closed. Kronos has run his ugly course. What were once the pride of Canadian wristwatches are now hard-to-find collectibles. What was once the mightiest retail establishment in the Dominion is now gone. Time (Kronos) has done his thing again.

The other word for time in Greek is "Kairos." It's most basic meaning is "the best time," an "opportune time," or the "optimal time for something to occur." I like the word "Kairos." It has a much better significance to me than its more famous counterpart. Its root meaning comes from archery. It refers to the point in space the arrow must travel through to hit its target. Thus Kairos refers to the exact point of space or time that one must travel through to reach his goal or target.

Remember General Joshua Lawrence Chamberlain, the hero of Little Round Top at the Battle of Gettysburg? Before serving in the military, he was a rhetoric professor in Maine at Bowdoin College. In rhetoric or homiletics, which I taught, we speak of a kairotic moment, the time in a speech when you really move an audience or congregation. It is that point in time when the speech or sermon is made or broken. It is the time the "arrow of speech" must move through to hit the rhetorical bull's-eye.

Chronos is inevitable. It marches on. We are all subject to its whims for both good and for deterioration. Kairos is neither inevitable nor to be taken for granted. Work hard not to miss the kairotic moments that come your way. Make the most of your opportunities. Be sensitive to those moments in time to reach out to those close to you. Be aware of the kairotic moments when those who are most important to you need you. God gives each one of us precious moments in time when we have opportunities to hit the bull's-eye!

You can't escape Chronos . . . you don't want to miss Kairos. ***Amen and Amen***

Plenty of Time?

Captain James Keith Boswell was the Chief Engineer for the Second Corp of the Army of Northern Virginia. Stonewall Jackson, perhaps one of the greatest of all American generals, was its commander. Captain Boswell was one of the youngest members of Jackson's brilliant staff. Captain Boswell was very gifted . . . he was an incurable romantic . . . and he was very much in love.

Captain James Keith Boswell (Photo in Public Domain)

You see, Captain James Boswell was totally possessed by his love for Miss Sophia de Butts of Fauquier County, Virginia. His concern was that he did not know if she returned those feelings. Captain Boswell's problem was that Miss de Butts was unaware of his affection.

Captain Boswell was in encampment with General Jackson that winter of 1862. Captain Boswell was losing it. Jedidiah Hotchkiss was his roommate and the chief topographical engineer on Jackson's staff. Hotchkiss was a brilliant cartographer whose work enabled Jackson to move his army swiftly and certainly. Hotchkiss was also losing it. His roommate would not quit talking and crying about his love. Hotchkiss had to do something.

Hotchkiss was great friends with General J.E.B. Stuart, himself an incurable romantic and ladies' man. Hotchkiss went to Stuart and told him how Boswell was driving him crazy with his all-night ruminations. Ever the cavalier, Stuart immediately became intrigued by this tale of unrequited love. Together they hatched a plan. Stuart agreed to send a letter to General Jackson requesting that Hotchkiss make him a map of Fauquier County. Hotchkiss was to lament to Jackson that he didn't know that territory well enough. Jackson was sure to express regret that they could not fill Stuart's request. Hotchkiss was to remind him that Boswell was from Fauquier County. Boswell could easily go home to sketch the needed map (and of course see his beloved Miss de Butts). Their plan was put into action. It worked perfectly. Much to his delight, Jackson sent Boswell to Fauquier County to prepare the map. As brilliant as the general was, he never knew his staff duped him. General Stuart, ever the romantic, was thrilled and quite proud of himself for such a good idea. Soon, however, a series of tragic events was about to occur. . .

The son of a well-respected Fauquier County family, Boswell had no problem arranging lodging at the spacious home of the de Butts family. There he was to discover that he had much competition for the love of the lovely Sophia. Boswell stayed there two weeks, surveying during the day and courting his love during the evenings. Perhaps courting is not the right word because the brave Captain had not yet told Sophia of his love, not even after two weeks! A young Fauquier county minister also was attempting to gain the love of Sophia. He often shared evenings with Boswell and her in the sitting room. They sang and made merry. Soon it became clear to the young minister that he was not to have her affection. One evening after some songs, the minister went upstairs in the de Butts home, put a gun to his head, and killed himself.

All present were stunned. Boswell felt that he was responsible for the death of the young minister. Sophia felt she was responsible. Tensions grew. Finally, three days after the tragedy, Captain Boswell could stand it no longer. Jackson had sent a messenger, requesting his return to camp. He had to act. He sat down with Sophia in her dining room. He poured out his love to her. He revealed all of his years of affection. Then, with greater fear than he ever had in facing a Union charge, Captain Boswell asked her if it would be possible for her to ever love him? "No, it will never be," was her dreaded answer.

Devastated, the young 24-year-old captain rode away. Prior to leaving, he angrily informed Miss de Butts that she would never see nor hear from him again. Back in camp Captain Boswell was worse off than ever. A week later, however, he was once again writing her of his love. He assured everyone that there was plenty of time for him to win her over. He was sure that one day she would truly come to love him. He would be very brave in battle and would win her heart.

In April 1863 the rival armies began to move. By May 1 they were poised against each other at the little crossroads of Chancellorsville, Virginia. Outnumbered and outgunned, Lee and Jackson decided on a desperate and bold strategy. Jackson, on an overnight secret march, would take his Corp around and out-flank General Joe Hooker's union forces. It was a dangerous and bold move. It worked brilliantly. By the afternoon of May 2, Jackson's troops had the union army in disarray.

Then one of the great tragedies of the war occurred. Riding to the front to scout the union position, General Stonewall Jackson was fatally wounded by excited infantry of his own Corp. The South had lost one of its greatest generals due to friendly fire. Lee said he had "lost his right arm." In the turmoil over the Jackson tragedy the fact was lost that a young member of Jackson's staff, riding with him, was also killed. Young Captain James Keith Boswell, chief engineer for the Second Corp of the Army of Northern Virginia, was shot twice through the heart, his body somersaulting over the front of his horse.

The Author with Boswell's Field Book - Notice Bullet Holes

The concern was so great over the general that no one thought of recovering young Boswell's body. Two days later, his best friend and roommate, Jed Hotchkiss, found his lifeless body. Hotchkiss carried it gently away and buried it in a small private cemetery near Chancellorsville. Hotchkiss was heart-broken. In one moment of time, he had lost his beloved general and his best friend.

Sophia de Butts eventually did fall in love. She married a young confederate colonel from Fauquier County. Hotchkiss went on to make great contributions to the Confederate cause.

The rest of his life Hotchkiss carried the pocket diary used by young Boswell at the time of his death. The diary was rendered almost unreadable by bullet holes. Two bullets had torn their way through it on the way to rendering the young captain's already-broken heart. The diary now resides in the Library of Congress archives along with 20,000 other items from the life of Jedediah Hotchkiss.

The story was long . . . its application will be brief. Often, we think we have time. Often we claim that someday we will accomplish this or that. Someday we will get around to it. "All in good time," we say. Like Captain Boswell, on his return from Fauquier County, we are confident that there is "plenty of time."

Take care of your priorities now. Don't let the important things go undone. Take care of those who you love. Never take time for granted. God, in His wisdom, knows our number of days. God, in His wisdom, doesn't reveal that knowledge to us.

Amen and Amen

Four Hundred Thirty-Seven Watches

Over the past year, 437 watches were found in the ruin of the world trade center towers. We often argue and debate which brand of watch is better. In this case, each of these 437 watches has a value and significance that far transcends its brand value. For each of these watches represents a person.

The meekest Timex is of the same value as the finest Patek. For each of these watches represents a person.

Some of them were stopped at the time of tragedy. Some of them were still ticking. Yet each was of equal value. For each of these watches represents a person.

Some were made of plastic, others of gold. Some were quartz-based, yet others were automatics. Yet each was of equal value. For each of these watches represents a person.

Sometimes I get really sad (and maybe a little angry) at the frivolous way we treat God. At times we turn God into our own personal puppet whose strings we pull for our own benefit. He becomes a straw man who we pull out when we are in trouble. Sometimes we relegate Him to a light-hearted being who we claim is on our side whether we are playing football, fighting a war, or arguing theology. When we curse, we use God's name. I often wonder why that is? When we score a touchdown we point to Him as if He has a role in that. We so often make light of God. We make Him into whatever we need or want Him to be at any given time.

And then on rare occasions . . . Time Stands Still. As a matter of fact, 437 watches stand still.

In those crystal clear moments of timelessness we often see God better. It is times when we are helpless and hopeless, when we do not and cannot understand; we begin to see God for who and what He is. September 11, 2001 was such an occasion. On that day and in the days that followed some of us got to know God a bit better.

Perhaps that is the saving grace in that pile of 437 watches. Perhaps in the midst of that heap of broken watches, some of us saw a timeless eternity.

Let us make a renewed commitment to acknowledging God . . . not as the cosmic clown who tickles our fancy . . . but as the timeless rock of ages, the shelter in the time of storm.

For each of these watches represents a person . . . and the loved ones left behind.

Amen and Amen

Taking a Break

I don't know about you all, but I am tired. This has been a very emotionally trying week. Phather Phil (my name on the watch forums) doesn't want to hear about all the pain and tragedy of 9-11 anymore. I don't want to hear any more about Iraq, terrorists on Alligator Alley, Florida elections, or customers who aren't paying their invoices. I think these are times where a lot of people are physically and emotionally tired. All the trials of the world are brought into our homes every day.

So there will be nothing deep, profound, or terribly meaningful in this week's homily. I think I will just relax. I think I am taking everything too seriously and too literally lately. What about you? Speaking of taking things literally, let me share with you one of my favorite map stories. As many of you know I enjoy studying maps. I see many great connections between maps and horology.

Here is a conversation that took place up in a balloon between Huckleberry Finn and Tom Sawyer. They were sailing along; not too sure where they were. The two were arguing whether or not the balloon they were drifting in was over Illinois or Indiana.

Huck: ...if we was going so fast we ought to be past Illinois, oughtn't we?

Tom: Certainly.

Huck: Well we ain't.

Tom: What's the reason we ain't?

Huck: I know by the color. We're right over Illinois yet. And you can see for yourself that Indiana ain't in sight.

Tom: I wonder what's the matter with you, Huck. You know by the color?

Huck: Yes I do.

Tom: What's the color got to do with it?

Huck: It's got everything to do with it. Illinois is green, Indiana is pink. You show me any pink down here, if you can. No sir; it's green.

Tom: Indiana pink? Why, what a lie?

Huck: It ain't no lie; I've seen it on the map, and it's pink.

(Mark Twain, *Tom Sawyer Abroad* (1894))

Maybe it's time for all of us to take a collective sigh, to back off a little. Maybe it's time for a good laugh. Perhaps it's time to call "time out," grab some of your favorite refreshment and tell a joke.

Poor ole Huck was mightily influenced by what he saw on a map. We get influenced by all the stimulus that bombards us every day.

I don't know about you, but Phather Phil is taking this Sunday off. I am going enjoy watching the Bucs (win or lose). I am not going to take the game too seriously. I am going to enjoy my family (and not take them too seriously either). I am not going to watch any news!

I am not going to worry about where I am or where I am going. I am just going to enjoy the balloon ride!

Amen and Amen

God's Promise . . . A Miracle of Love

For this week's homily, I would like to share with you an article I wrote twenty years ago. Just this week, my wife found it tucked away in an old chest. I had forgotten writing it. I hope you all don't mind a personal story. This article was published in 1983. That was a long time ago. Yet, the lessons that I learned those long twenty years past are still at work in my life. To my knowledge, there is no watch that measures time in twenty-year increments. It seems like a hundred years ago. It also seems like yesterday. . . .

God's Promise: A Miracle of Love

"Oh, look; he just fits!" Such simple words. Yet, so very powerfully are they locked into my mind. You see, those were the first words I remember ever hearing about my son. Those simple words were to absolutely transform my world. They launched me on the greatest journey of my life. They introduced me to God in a new and special way. They introduced me to my wife, to myself, and to my son in a new and special way. As I think about the incident, my eyes mist and my heart swells with deep, silent gratitude.

"Oh, look; he just fits!" I had just finished performing a wedding for a friend of mine; a lovely outdoor wedding in May of 1978. The air was filled with the fragrance of flowers. Bees buzzed about their business as the final "I do's" were exchanged. The service was over and I went looking for my wife. I found her on the front lawn, holding a tiny baby in her arms. The wife of a colleague of mine stood by her side. An empty stroller sat on the lawn in front of her.

As I approached, the ladies looked up. The friend beamed and brightly chirped, "Oh, look; he just fits!" She went on, "He's a perfect fit in Jeanne's arms! Baby Chris and I just had a conversation. He told me he'd like his last name to be Stover!"

Anger welled up inside me. My wife was always holding babies. I didn't like it. I didn't like babies. I didn't like someone egging my wife on about children. Children were a sore enough subject for us. Besides all that, this baby was particularly scrawny and unresponsive. I wasn't the least bit impressed.

Sensing my discomfort, our friend, three-month-old Christopher's foster mother apologized and assured us she was just teasing. She explained that Christopher was a disabled baby, a ward of the state who had been declared "unadoptable" by the physicians. Chris had a rare syndrome, a combination of birth defects and prematurity. He was blind, profoundly retarded, had little muscle tone, and probably would die before the age of three from failure to thrive. As far as the doctors were concerned, he was bound for a state institution for infants.

Unadoptable. That was fine with me. I didn't like kids anyway. At least, I tried not to like them. I had tried not liking them ever since 1973, when my wife had a cantaloupe-sized tumor removed during surgery that left her unable to have children.

It is amazing how differently people respond to the same hurt. My wife reacted by surrounding herself with children. She taught school, volunteered to supervise the church nursery, and generally played with or held every child she saw. My response was the opposite; I distanced myself from children at every opportunity. I grew irritated when Jeanne became involved with every child who walked or crawled near her. She tried to fulfill her unmet need with others' children. I tried to deny that the need existed. I ignored children. Neither approach really worked.

Later during the reception, I remember walking over to the stroller (when no one was around, of course) to look at the sleeping baby. I had never seen such a small, frail child. I was awed by his vulnerability. His unfocusing eyes rolled back up in his head. Unfocusing? Yes. But, oh, so blue! On top of his tiny head a forest of blond hair glowed in the sunlight. Having blue eyes and blond hair myself, I really could not think of a better combination! I remember being incensed at two or three yellow jackets that buzzed around those unseeing eyes. Instinctively I lashed out at them with my hand. How could they dare bother such a helpless little boy?

Here was a tiny baby, weak and extremely helpless, posing no threat to my hurt. I allowed him to touch me deeply that afternoon. After all, he was safe. He was unadoptable.

My wife and I had discussed adoption. It was not an easy topic for us. How could we find a perfect, healthy young baby to adopt? They were so scarce and waiting lists were so long. Waiting and hoping only increased the risk of hurt. No, adoption was not the answer. For me, my wall of isolation from children was much safer.

During that entire year, I had been involved in a widespread preaching-teaching ministry. The focus of my teaching had been on Christ's unconditional love for us. Now God used the same message to convict me. How could I demand that a baby be perfect before I would love him, when Christ so freely gave His love when I was yet a sinner? Phil Stover, imperfect, handicapped by sin and ego, spiritually near blind and retarded was met with Christ's unconditional love over and over. The more I heard it the more assured I became of following God's direction for us concerning Chris.

Not long after that May afternoon, we began the difficult adoption process. At first, doctors would not allow Chris to be adopted. Their minds had to be changed. After this was accomplished, the state said we could not adopt him because we were not on their waiting list. In getting him declared adoptable, we had ruled ourselves out. Our hearts sank. But after three months of waiting, the social worker disqualified everyone else with an interest in Chris. On August 1, 1978, Christopher came to live in our home. The week before was a blur of garage sales and flea markets. I never dreamed how much stuff was needed for a baby. We started out as his foster parents, but in October 1979 the final court order was signed. He was at last our son. I was never to be the same.

Many of our greatest spiritual lessons are not learned in a church pew; they are learned in life. As we launch out by faith into the unknown, God blesses. Spiritual growth involves risk-taking. Real faith involves a willingness to leap into the unknown. Many do not grow. They prefer the security of established mental and emotional sanctuaries to the uncharted regions of growth. I know that before Chris, my ministry was successful, yet inside I was filled with the sin of self-centeredness. I ministered, yes, to meet my own needs. I was grateful but proud when people responded to my preaching. I gave God part of the glory but kept some of it for myself. Then came Chris, and I experienced real growth.

After we adopted him, the doctors found that, in addition to all his other problems, he also was autistic. Our hearts broke. Nevertheless, we worked very hard with Chris. My wife quit teaching and devoted all of her energy to nurturing him. We prayed with and for Chris. Bit by bit, ever so slowly change came. Each tiny step in his development broke like a rainbow into our lives. As he developed, our marriage developed. As Chris grew, I grew. I found myself humbly, quietly thanking God for His overwhelming goodness to us. I didn't deserve it. God just kept giving us special miracles in and through our special son.

In my life, I have been blessed by two extra-special gifts from God: His son and my son. On his third birthday, the one the doctors said he would never reach, we had quite a party. Christopher is now five years old. He can see, run, and play much like any other five-year-old boy. Medical problems still exist, but so do the miracles. He is my son. I love him so.

I'm still growing too! I've learned that only through active faith can one truly grow in the spirit of Christ. Each of us must be willing to take a risk and leap out by faith to receive God's very special gifts.

Chris is now twenty-four years old. He is doing so well. We are proud of all his growth and grateful to God for bringing him into our lives.

Time doesn't change our deepest emotions and experiences. When it comes to the deepest parts of our lives, time is really irrelevant.

Twenty years ago? Nah, it can't be that long. It seems like just a moment in time ago!

Amen and Amen

The Loss of a Parent

Today we on the watch forum learned the sad news that one of our own lost a parent. At the news of such a loss, our forum immediately switches gears, becoming a community. Many messages of condolences are posted. Heart-felt wishes and prayers are posted.

I never met the lady. I only met her son once, for a few days last October in Lancaster. Yet, I know that she was a wonderful lady. She raised a son who cares, has a wonderful sense of humor, is loyal to his friends, is generous, and is a wonderful example to us all in so many ways. She must have been all of that and more. Through her modeling, she must have helped instill those virtues in her son.

Today, earth is a poorer place and heaven is much richer.

Many of us are at the age where we either have or shortly will experience the loss of our parents. Both of mine are gone. They were good people, however full of faults and short-comings. They cared passionately about their faith. They worked hard, argued hard, laughed hard, got on my nerves hard, and never stopped parenting me until the day they died in their eighties.

Mine are gone. Perhaps yours are still alive. You are now busy, occupied with your own family. Perhaps you have hurts, anger, or pain from some time in your youth or adulthood where they upset you. Perhaps you are not as close to them as you once were. Maybe you have never been close.

Let me simply, in honor of Tom's mom, encourage you to phone home. If there is hurt, heal it. If there is distance, close it. If there are wrongs, forgive them. Work at it. Love your spouse, your kids, and your folks. They gave you life. Perhaps in re-building your relationship with them, or simply phoning them, you can now bring life to them as well.

Tom . . . we honor your mom, because she helped make you the man you are, a good man.

Check out your watches . . . see what time it is. Maybe it is time to emotionally, spiritually, and/or physically go home.

Amen and Amen

Scrapple, Shoo-fly Pie, and Watches

For today's homily, I would like to give you a bit of the background on one of Switzerland's most famous products. When one thinks of Switzerland, cheese, the Alps, and watches immediately come to mind.

For some of us, the most fascinating product of Switzerland is none of the above. In a few weeks at Convergence (a meeting of watch enthusiasts held twice in Pennsylvania), many of the readers of this forum will come face-to-face for perhaps the first time, with this famous Swiss export.

Central and East-Central Pennsylvania are home to one of the largest concentration of Anabaptists in the world. For the most part, the Anabaptist community is made up of believers in the various Brethren, Mennonite, and Amish churches. There are Anabaptists in virtually every state in the U.S. There are millions worldwide. All together, they form one of the largest Swiss exports!

The Anabaptist movement began prior to the reformation, but is typically dated to around 1525 or so. In Switzerland they became known as Swiss Brethren. They were initially a part of the early reformation. They soon split from other Protestant reformers as leaders like Zwingli and Calvin became increasingly militaristic in their attitudes. As the Protestant and Catholic armies of Swiss cantons fought each other in the sixteenth and seventeenth centuries the Swiss Brethren became increasingly estranged from both. Anabaptists were banned from all parts of Switzerland, especially their original home, that of Berne Canton. Anabaptists believed in adult baptism, pacifism, and the refusal to take oaths of allegiance to any earthly state. As Catholicism and Protestantism became increasingly state controlled, Swiss Brethren became increasingly marginalized. Swiss Brethren were increasingly subject to death by drowning (mocking their baptism beliefs), banning, and being sold as slaves to the Venetian galleys. Both sides of the religious conflicts persecuted them. In fact, laws were on the books until the nineteenth century in Switzerland allowing Anabaptists to be killed or enslaved. The French Revolution was of great help to the Anabaptists. It totally changed the governance structure in Switzerland and persecution eased.

Because of the danger, many Swiss Brethren migrated to Germany and the Netherlands. Many were taken by force from the Berne area and forced onto boats to go to America. Many eventually went to Russia. They were hard working and honest people who were often welcomed by monarchs needing a ready work force. In the 18th, 19th, and 20th century, for many reasons, large groups migrated elsewhere. As pressures increased on German speaking Anabaptists in Russia, many migrated to Canada, the western U.S., Uruguay, Paraguay, and Mexico. Russian Anabaptists extensively populated the northern plains states of the U.S. WWI was very hard on these people.

Many Anabaptists immigrated to Pennsylvania. William Penn encouraged this. There they prospered and established missions to other areas (Florida and Virginia for example). Today the largest Mennonite university is in Virginia and 1 out of 8 people in Sarasota County, Florida is Amish, Mennonite, or Brethren. Fresno, California is home to thousands of Anabaptists. Today there are more Mennonites of color around the world than there are Caucasian.

The Amish are among the most conservative of the main Anabaptist communities. They separated from the Mennonites in the early 1700's. They speak Pennsylvania Dutch (a low dialect of German) among themselves. They have legal protection for their young people to go to school only through the eighth grade. They tolerate their cult status as a tourist curiosity. You will more than likely see their buggies in Lancaster County while you are there. The buggies may be from conservative Brethren groups as well. If you see Amish, you might want to ask before taking pictures. They will appreciate having the opportunity to say no. Mennonites tend to separate theologically, but not socially. Brethren are all over the barn (good pun, huh?). Women wear prayer coverings. You can often tell the group the ladies come from by the form and color of their covering. Some only wear them to church, some all the time, and some not at all. For an outsider, ("English," to the Amish) it is very hard to distinguish between conservative Amish and Brethren.

The Anabaptist community is not a monolithic community. Most of them are conscientious objectors, don't believe in taking oaths and are not overly patriotic (comes from having to move from country to country over the years). They also focus on heaven as the kingdom to which they should be loyal. In Lancaster County you will find Amish, Brethren, and Mennonites. To the trained eye it is easy to distinguish between them. They join together in their theology, which is primarily Arminian in its beliefs. They love music, crafts, and their foods. You will never eat better than in Pennsylvania Dutch (their language and culture) restaurants. Lots of pork, cabbages, and wonderful deserts! They are very proud of their history and will talk for hours about the martyrdom of their ancestors. The Lancaster County Anabaptists are mostly of Swiss heritage. Russian Anabaptists are mostly in the western U.S., Canada, and Kansas.

Since this is a horological homily, let me insert here that quite a few Mennonites worked in the Hamilton factory in Lancaster over the years. Jewelry was and in many cases, still is forbidden. Watches, especially Hamilton were the exception. Many brides receive watches instead of rings at engagement time. A Mennonite uncle and nephew in the Jura Region of Switzerland even have their own watch brand, MenSim watches. They are very popular among the Mennonite community here in the U.S. They are not very good watches; mostly quartz movements in cheap cases (don't tell anyone I said that!).

Enjoy the wonderful culture of Lancaster. It is an increasingly diverse town. The Anabaptists remain, however the focal point of its tourist attractions. Just please remember, the Anabaptists of Lancaster County are not attractions in a park. They are real people living in the place they call home. Be sensitive in that as you interact with them.

I am happy to answer any questions about the Anabaptists that you may have at Convergence. You see, I am an Anabaptist! I taught Mennonite history at the collegiate level and am a licensed Mennonite minister. I was the headmaster of a large Mennonite K-12 school. My wife's great grandfather was a Mennonite bishop in Kansas. She is a pure blood Swiss Mennonite, ranking her high in the Mennonite pecking order. Our family belongs to Bahia Vista Mennonite Church here in Sarasota, one of the largest Mennonite churches in the United States.

I even have an Amish Buggy Watch! (Photo by Author)

Finally, the history of the Anabaptist community is a sad one, full of persecution, slavery, and martyrdom. Next to those of the Jewish faith, more Anabaptists were killed in WWII than any other single faith group (because of their faith). Protestants and Catholics persecuted them alike from the 15th through the 20th centuries.

Much tragedy has been wrought in the name of religion. We all know that. I don't need to dwell on that. May the presence of the "quiet in the land" (as Anabaptists like to call themselves) remind us all of the evil that has been done in the name of religion. Sometimes I think God must cry at the things done in His name. Let us take Convergence and the chance it offers to bring us up close and personal with these simple people as a time to re-dedicate ourselves to peace, tolerance, and respect. I think that will make God smile!

Enjoy Convergence! Enjoy the scrapple and shoo-fly pie!

Amen and Amen

Losing Your Balance . . . Wheel

Several months ago I became very enthusiastic about pocket watches. I did a lot of research and bought an English fusee watch dating from the mid-19th century. I was very excited. It arrived promptly and was much more substantial than I had anticipated. I was very excited because it was my first fusee chain watch! That was good.

I wound it from the back and set it from the front (a key does both). It didn't work! I was very sad. That was bad. I posted on the NAWCC Pocket Watch forum, asking some questions about it not working. All the experts assured me it was authentic and all original. That was good. They gave me lots of different ideas on what might be wrong and on how to fix it. That was bad. They all agreed it was a very nice watch and probably only a minor problem from shipping. The seller assured me it was working when it left England.

One gentleman, an English Fusee expert named Oliver Mundy, was very helpful. That was good. He suggested I take a picture of the movement and send it to him. Upon opening the back of the hunter case, I discovered a dust cover hiding the movement. That was bad. A few members of the forum assured me that such a watch does not have a dust cover. Others agreed, so what was this strange looking thing?

Now, I have never before taken a dust cover (for that is indeed what it was) off a fusee pocket watch movement. I saw a curved slit cut into the dust cover that seemed to indicate the dust cover would rotate and easily come off once it was released from the movement. That made perfect sense to me. I checked it all out and proceeded with the minor effort of removing one small screw from the dust cover. I removed the screw with my trusty jeweler's screwdriver. Everything in the world was wonderful. One little screw appeared to be holding the dust cover on and nothing else. The result certainly wasn't good. The dust cover? Oh yes it did indeed come off! That was good. However, the balance wheel also came off too. That was bad. The hairspring also came off. That was worse than bad.

You see on this particular watch the balance cock holds down the balance wheel, which holds down the hairspring. See how smart I am? The little screw I unscrewed? It has nothing to do with the dust cover. It holds the balance cock to a bridge that holds the balance wheel that in turn holds the hairspring in place. The dust cover? It just slides on a rivet type thing and comes right off! Easy as pie; shoo-fly pie that is!!

So what made the watch not work in the first place? We will never know because the balance cock is now off, the balance wheel is now off, and the hairspring resembles the tangle of hair left on the drain from shampooing my hair. Yes I am getting that old; that is bad! So now I have a wonderful rare English Fusee pocket watch that is in shambles. All from one little screw! One tiny little mistake! One really messed up watch!

Now, where is the homily in all this? It may seem more like a Greek tragedy (or comedy – depending on the nature of your sense of humor)! Well, sometimes in life we don't mean to do bad things. We don't mean to make mistakes. We have no intention of making a mess out of things. But sometimes we do. One seemingly innocent action ends up hurting someone, something, or yourself. The damage from an error is not always a function of the intent. Sometimes we do little things wrong that have big consequences.

When you do something that you don't intend and it has negative consequences, don't bother justifying your error. Don't waste the time explaining that your intent was good. When you foul up, own up to it. Learn from your error and do your best not to make the same mistake again. Be honest about it. Don't blame others or the innocence of your intent. And try and keep a smile through it all.

My wife thinks that sometimes I have a few screws loose. In this case she is absolutely correct!

One more thing about Mr. Oliver Mundy, remember him? He offered to fix the watch for me at no cost. This Good Samaritan in Cornwall, England is now repairing it. Bless him. He has taken pity on this bumbling Yankee watch destroyer. Mr. Oliver Mundy is a good man.

The hairspring connected to the balance wheel; the balance wheel connected to the balance cock; the balance cock connected to the little screw; now hear the word of the Lord!!

Amen and Amen

Passing the Sun Test

Clock from Jackson Site - National Park Service

It is the clock that was in the room in May of 1863 when legendary Confederate General Stonewall Jackson died from wounds received at the battle of Chancellorsville. Folklore says that when he died at 3:15 p.m. that Sunday afternoon, the clock stopped running. I don't really believe that. But I have had an interest in and a curiosity about that clock.

Some research informed me that it is a Brewster Ingraham Connecticut-made clock from around 1850. It is styled a "gothic" clock. The clock is still in the room where he died. It was given to the National Park Service in 1933. They maintain the Jackson Shrine in Guinea Station, VA. There, on May 10, 1863, in a small room with just an easy chair, a bed, and the mantel clock, Jackson died. Only the bed and clock remain. The National Park Service informs all visitors that they are the exact same clock and bed used by the general during his week's stay there.

My interest in both Jackson and clocks has even led me to try and find a similar clock to purchase for my office. I found one not too long ago on EBay. I quit long before the bidding rose into the thousands of dollars. The clock is not rare, but the connection with Jackson drives the price up!

About a month ago, I was told by a poster on the NAWCC (National Association of Watch and Clock Collectors) clock forum that the NAWCC Bulletin had published an article in a recent edition on this very same clock. I soon was visiting their museum in Columbia, PA and as soon as we had free time there I tore into the library, asked the librarian and was quickly given the right Bulletin. I made a copy of the article, tucked it into my pocket, and quickly got lost amongst all the goodies in the museum.

I did not read the article until I got back to Sarasota. It was well written, very informative, and very disappointing. Upon reading the article, I felt that the wind had been taken out of me. Why so?

Well, the article discussed the clock in some detail. Remember, the National Park Service indicates that it is the exact clock on the exact mantle and in the exact location as it was the day Jackson died. The Bulletin article indicates that the hands are not original. The dial is not original. The tablet (glass front) is not original. The movement is not original. The case back is not original. It is plywood. The article went on to say that the movement and dial are from a very inexpensive 1890's Ingraham kitchen clock! Somewhere in the late 1890's or early 1900's, someone replaced just about everything but the basic case.

Learning all this has really burst my bubble. I am very disappointed. There was something a bit nostalgic and romantic (especially to a watch, clock, and civil war enthusiast) about looking at a clock that had played a role in history, only to find out that most of it came from someone's late nineteenth century kitchen clock! I felt deceived.

Then just yesterday I began reflecting on the clock. I began wondering about authenticity. I wonder if I am something like that clock? When people look at me are they seeing a truly authentic person? Or am I merely the shell of the person I claim to be? I want to be the kind of person whose insides are consistent with my outer representation to the world. I truly hope there is more genuineness and sincerity about me than my outer shell. I truly hope I am more authentic than the clock currently sitting on that mantle in Guinea Station, VA.

The word sincere is actually a Latin word, meaning "without wax." The term implies "sun tested." The ancients fired their fine porcelain in kilns, and sometimes in the process of firing, cracks appeared in the finished product. Dishonest merchants smeared wax over these cracks and tried to pass them off as flawless porcelain. That worked, unless the pieces were held up to the light of the sun. Honest merchants would declare their wares to be *sine cera or* "without wax."

The Greek equivalent word for sincerity is *elekrine*. It comes from two words *helios* - sun and *krine* - to test. The same pottery metaphor is used.

Carl Rogers, the great American psychologist said that we all have an ideal self (how we would like to be perceived by ourselves and others) and a phenomenological or real self (how we actually are). The more congruent the two are the greater likelihood of our living a happy and healthy life.

How about you? Does your life pass the sun test? Is your life "without wax?"

I was disappointed by what I learned about the famous Jackson clock. Upon reflection however, what I have learned about it has reminded me of something very important. My life is on a mantle for all to see. I pray that when they look at me, they see an authentic person, both inside and out.

Amen and Amen

Singing Life's Songs

In my years of buying and selling watches I have learned that each movement sings its own song. The big pocket watch movement sings its slow and steady song. Its regular beat is reassuring and firm. The pocket watch sings its song for all to hear.

The El Primero sings the fastest song of all. Its 36,000 beats per hour is the rock and roll song of watch movements. It is exciting. Sometimes its song even has to be slowed down a bit. It sings the heavy metal music of watches

The quartz watch is silent. Its song is the in the quiet sounds of silence. It is known for its accuracy and dependability more than for its song. Being silent is, of itself, neither good nor bad. Joseph, the earthly father of Jesus did not have one recorded word in scripture. He never says a word, but is a good and faithful father and husband. Like the quartz watch, he is known more for his faithfulness than his words. His actions are his song.

My favorite watch song is that of the tuning fork movement. It sings a steady and constant song. Its range is not broad but it sure does sing a constant humming vigilance. Like the individual whose song is always evident, the tuning fork needs no winding. It just sings and sings.

I believe also that God has given each one of us a song. Our songs are as individual and different as the songs of the watches. Some of us are slow and steady. Some sing with a passion that sometimes has to be slowed down. We are all different. We move to different rhythms with different needs and desires.

Even our best friends don't sing the same song we do. Some years ago I wrote this poem, using the metaphor of Pooh and Piglet (best friends in the Hundred Aker Woods) to show how different even best friend's songs may be:

The Hope of Spring

Pooh yawned a big yawn, a worried look on his brow,
Snows falling, he's not bright, but knew the time was now.
Rare did Pooh fret, 'cept when the hunny jar was low,
His long winter's nap, he knew it's past time to go.

Now, Piglet and Pooh were the best friends in the land.
They strolled through the hundred-aker wood, hand-in-hand.
Best of friends, souls as one, yet so different you know,
Pigs sleep for a night—bears for the whole winter's snow.

Through tears at their parting, Pooh cried, "Come nap with me."
Deep in his hunny brain he knew it just couldn't be.
Piglet cried, "I love you so, don't go to your lair.
Piglet raged, "Just go, leave me. I really don't care.

"I'll dream of you, Piglet, 'til my hand you do hold".
"I'll watch o'er your den, Pooh, through the months that are cold."
Parting angry or in peace depends on one thing,
Whether they choose to believe in the hope of spring.

Pooh and Piglet were best friends yet each had their own individual song.

Sometimes in the stress and strain of life we forget the words and notes of our song. There are times when life brings us so low that we lose sight of the joy that God has put within us. The cause may be of our own doing, or no fault of our own, but many of us come to the point where we stop singing.

My favorite definition of love is that we get to know someone so well that we learn their song and then sing it back to them when they have forgotten the words. We all need people in our lives who from time to time remind us of our uniqueness, our potential, our song. Loving someone enough to help them to sing again is a great joy and an even greater privilege.

May we each be prepared to be there for someone close to us who needs to remember his or her song. There is perhaps no greater joy than to remind someone of the words and tune of his or her own special melody. And please don't forget your own song, the one that makes you a unique and special individual.

After returning to Florida from Lancaster, I wrote this poem. It reflects my sincere belief in the song.

The Song

We each have a song, yet none are the same.
The tune, rhyme, and words - our heart's burning flame.
The song's a fire that can dim and grow cold
When life's out of tune, the words seem so old.

God gave me a song of my very own.
You knew me before, when the sun still shone.
But I forget the words and melody.
In love, won't you sing my song back to me?

Our lives so stressed, no one sings anymore.
So lost out at sea, we long for the shore.
When we sing, it's a solo . . .only me . . .
When singing alone, there's no harmony.

God gave me a song of my very own.
You knew me before, when the sun still shone.
But I forget the words and melody.
In love, won't you sing my song back to me?

Your love is the hope that I'll sing again.
The goal of my life and my prayer's amen.
To love is to learn the other's life song.
Singing it back to them when all's gone wrong.

God gave me a song of my very own.
You knew me before, when the sun still shone.
But I forget the words and melody.
In love, won't you sing my song back to me?

When we each find our song . . . our heart's desire . . .
Join voices as one . . . the whole human choir.
Praise to the Singer who gives us the song.
Thanks to the lovers who make us belong.

God gave me a song of my very own.
You knew me before, when the sun still shone.
But I forget the words and melody.
In love, won't you sing my song back to me?

In love, won't you sing my song back to me?

Amen and Amen

What Watches Tell About Life

I am sure that no one in this room has any doubt about the ability of watches to tell us the correct time. That is a given. My desire tonight is not to expound on how watches tell time; my interest is in sharing what they tell me about life.

I have been collecting, buying and selling watches for about seven years now. Richard Paige of Timezone sold me the first two watches I bought consciously as a collector around Christmas 1995. They were two wonderful Oris watches. However, by Easter of the next year, they were both gone. I was well on my way to an addiction of profound proportions; a sickness which the vast majority of us in this room share.

I have known the prolonged hunt for that one perfect watch that I just had to have. Only to sell it to fund the next got-to-have watch and so on and so on. I have even gone so far as to buy back a watch that I had previously owned. One time I didn't even remember having owned it until the seller told me he had bought it from me. This is truly a disease of epidemic proportion. Perhaps I should more appropriately start out my homily by confessing:

"Hi, my name is Phil. I am a watchaholic." No 12 or 20 step program will cure this disease. I stand before you wearing the one watch I have owned that I have never even considered selling, the EOT Collaboration I. This watch means more to me than its ability to tell time. To me it represents the fellowship, cooperation, and friendship of a great bunch of addicts who are just like me, the members of the EOT Watch Discussion Forum. I salute you each and every one.

What has collecting watches taught me?

1. The Value of a Watch is not in the price paid, but in the pleasure perceived. Thus it is with so much of life. An event does not have to cost a lot to be precious to those participating. A simple thing can mean much more than its expensive counterpart. My $10.00 Sears Winnie the Pooh watch is one of my very favorite. I really enjoy the Winnie the Pooh stories and this is the only automatic movement Pooh watch I have ever seen. Combine it all together and you have a $10 watch with a lot of meaning. The value found in a watch may also be transient. There are many more things in life whose value is more permanent. I can't wait to receive a watch recently bought. In six months it may be gone, its value now placed in the next "can't wait" acquisition. There is little permanence in the hobby; in life hopefully we value what is important and maintain that appreciation over time.

Sears Winnie the Pooh Watch (Photo by Author)

2. Burdens can indeed at times be blessings in disguise. Sometimes the burdens keep us going.

There's a story about an old grandfather clock that had stood for three generations in the same corner of a room, faithfully ticking off the minutes and hours, day after day. In the clock was a heavy weight that the owner pulled to the top each night to keep it running. Then one day the clock was sold, and the new owner noticed the heavy weight. "Too bad," he said, "that such an old clock should have to bear so great a load." So he took the weight off the chain. At once the clock stopped ticking. "Why did you do that?" asked the clock. "I wanted to lighten your burden," said the man. "Please put it back," said the clock. "That's what keeps me going!"

3. There is no direct correlation between the worth of an individual and the worth of his or her watches. Possessions don't tell the value of the person. While the worth of a watch may be correlated to its rarity and the complexity of its movement; that of a person is correlated to lives impacted in a positive manner, to the simplicity of the life lived, and to the integrity demonstrated over time and in different situations.

4. We are each very different. We have different tastes and preferences. That is OK because we learn from each other and get to appreciate varying approaches to collecting watches. I am unique: I know of no one else who collects map dial watches. I know of only a few who like private label pocket watches. I like watches with orange dial, of course I like anything orange, including oranges!

An Orange Seiko "Monster" (Photo by Author)

I really like two tone bracelets and watches. Many of you wouldn't consider buying a watch with that feature. I really don't like dates on watches. Many wouldn't buy a watch without one. These differences help me to look at things from another's perspective. They show me other perspectives, no better or worse than my own. I have spent time living in other countries where other cultures predominate. So it is with watch collecting; we learn to appreciate perspectives different from our own.

There are lessons to be learned everywhere in life. I trust you will commit to letting life: your work, your hobby, your family, and all its other aspects teach you lessons to make you a more complete person.

Amen and Amen

The Clock That Couldn't Tell Time

Young Benjamin was at that age. Sometimes he was twelve years young. Sometimes he was twelve years old. You were never sure which. Benjamin did what all twelve year old boys do . . . he just did it all a little bit more. He dropped things. He tripped over things. His feet had outgrown his body. He was "too old" to act that way. He was "too young" to act this way. Poor Benjamin was never sure how to act. Like many middle schoolers, Benjamin was a sweet and sensitive kid who would die if anyone thought that about him. Not good at sports and very shy . . . Benjamin pretty much kept things inside.

Benjamin's dad was a good man who was out of work. Christmas was coming. Things were pretty tense at home. It was the kind of tense where everyone is unsure about everything. That is the worst kind of tense, because you're never sure where or when it might erupt. The family: Benjamin, mom, dad, and his sister needed money. Dad knew it, so he began to look around the house for things to sell. He wanted his family to have a nice Christmas. That "want" just added to his burden. He sometimes felt that without providing for his family, he was useless. Wanting to provide, being embarrassed, and feeling useless; add them all up and you've got a recipe for tension.

One evening dad got out the old family clock and set it on the dining room table. It had been his father's and his father's father's. He knew it had to be worth some money. He hadn't set it for years. He wasn't even sure it still worked. He had never used an online auction, but he had heard that people often pay a lot for old clocks.

The old key that wound it was taped to the back. Benjamin's dad pulled it off, stuck it in the hole in front of the clock, and tried to turn it. Nothing happened. The key wouldn't turn no matter how hard he tried. He tried so hard, the key got stuck in the little hole. The clock didn't work . . . the clock couldn't tell time. He couldn't sell it if it didn't work. Dad remembered how his father used to lovingly wind it when he was a boy. He had loved listening to its chime. He thought it was the nicest sound he had ever heard. Full of mixed emotions about it not working, he wasn't sure how to feel. Sometimes when someone isn't sure how to feel, they feel the first thing . . . in this case anger and frustration.

Right in the middle of those feelings, Benjamin bounded into the room. If you ever have known a middle-schooler, you know they never walk anywhere. They bound or they bounce. They never walk. Benjamin bounced into the dining room, tripped over his own feet and crumbled into a heap in front of his father. It was bad timing . . . really bad timing. Benjamin crashed. The key caught. Dad complained. Before he could stop them, the words were out of his mouth, "This clock can't keep time . . . it isn't worth anything!" Looking down at this son, he added "and neither are you!" The sting of the words was worse than that of any wasp. Silence filled the room. Benjamin ran out. Dad bowed his head over his mean words. Words spoken in anger can never be taken back. Dad didn't know how to fix his own work situation, the clock, or his son's pain. Lately, it seemed like he couldn't fix anything. Dad was silent in pain. Benjamin was silent in grief. Dad silently put the old now-broken clock back in the closet.

Benjamin never thought he was worth much. Now his dad had confirmed it. It is one thing to think it. It is another altogether to hear it from someone you love. The impact was devastating. This twelve-year old boy, owner of so little self-confidence, had even less now. Yet . . . Benjamin almost - sort of understood. He really loved his dad. He knew things were bad. He just didn't know how to make it better. There was nothing he could do to help. Yet, he wanted to with everything that was in him. He thought and thought until his thinker hurt. He laid up on his bed trying to figure out how to help make things better. After what seemed like an eternity (especially for a twelve-year old), Benjamin came up with an idea.

He didn't have much money, but he knew what he was going to do. Every day, as he walked to school, he went past an old house. In front of that house was an even older sign that said *"**Watch and Clock Repair**."* Benjamin had never seen anyone there, but he had bounded by that sign a thousand times. He knew how much his dad loved that old clock. He would take it to that old house. He would get the clock fixed. His dad would be proud of him. He was only twelve. He couldn't get a full-time job. He could, however, get that clock fixed and hopefully it would run like it did when his dad was his age.

Benjamin waited for his dad to leave the dining room. He ran in (of course!), opened the closet, and tucked the clock under his arm. Running (of course!) out the door he shivered as the cold air hit him. Christmas was only a few weeks away. He didn't have time to go back in and get a jacket. It wasn't that far anyway. Running (you didn't expect anything else did you?) up the walkway of the old house, Benjamin came to a screeching stop. All his twelve-year old insecurity came to the surface. What if he didn't have enough money? What if the clock person was mean? Twelve-year old boys are full of "what ifs." Pausing at that front door, they almost overwhelmed Benjamin's determination. Almost . . . but not quite. With uncharacteristic bravery, Benjamin buzzed the bell.

After the longest while, just as Benjamin was ready to leave, the door cracked open. There standing in front of Benjamin was the living incarnation of Santa Claus (except this man was much skinnier!). Silver hair, a silver beard, a really kind smile, and bright eyes peered out at him. "Can I help you young man?" Benjamin liked being called anything with "man" in it. It made him feel grown up. Benjamin was so full of looking at the old man, he almost forgot to answer. The cold was beginning to get to him and he started shivering from cold and uncertainty. Uncertainty is the domain of middle-school boys. Benjamin was the king of that domain.

"Sir," he stammered as the man waited patiently, "I saw your sign and I need to get this clock fixed." The clockmaker studied him. Here was a boy on a mission. He was also sure the boy needed to come in out of the cold. "Please, come on in," said the stranger. "I am a clockmaker, perhaps I can help you." Benjamin was freezing. He put aside all caution and entered the man's house. As his eyes adjusted to the darkness, he could make out what seemed like millions of clocks . . . cuckoo clocks, tall case clocks, shelf clocks . . . clocks of every size and description. "My shop has been closed for years," said the clockmaker. "I just never bothered to take that old sign down." Then, touched by the boy's sincerity, he repeated, "How can I help you?"

Trembling, Benjamin showed him the clock. "Please sir, I need to have this clock fixed. It is my dad's clock and it is broken. Can you please help it to tell time? It's very important!" The clockmaker saw that it was a very nice old mantle clock, a 19th century Ingraham from Connecticut. "Well, let's see," as he put his glasses on. Examining the clock, he quickly decided that he could fix it. "Leave it here with me and I will fix it for you." Relieved, Benjamin asked "how much will it cost?" Sensing the boy's sincerity, the clockmaker simply said "we'll worry about that later. You come by in a couple of days and we will talk about it."

Benjamin was thrilled. The old man was very nice. He didn't talk to him like most grown-ups talk to kids. He couldn't wait for the "couple of days" to be over. Three days later, Benjamin was once again buzzing the doorbell. The old man answered the door and let Benjamin in. Smiling, he led Ben over to his workbench. This scene was repeated day after day for the next two weeks. Benjamin loved visiting the clockmaker. He had never seen such wonderful tools. He sat quietly (a real feat for a twelve-year old) as the old man worked on "their" clock.

Day after day, during the Christmas vacation, he spent time at the clockmaker's, as the old man took the clock apart and put it back together; every gear, every lever, every step of the way fascinated the young boy. The old man never fussed at his questions. He didn't complain about being watched. It was as if he knew how important it was to Benjamin to be treated like who he was . . . a bright intelligent and sometimes "off-the-wall" twelve year old. Thousands of questions brought just as many answers. Soon, the clock was almost done. Just as important, Benjamin had found a real friend.

A few days before Christmas, the kind clockmaker said to Benjamin, "You better go home now; tomorrow the clock will be done! I will bring it by your house." In a few short weeks, Benjamin had grown to love the old man. No one had ever been so kind and patient with him.

Back at home, things were a little better. Benjamin's dad had found a temporary job. He wasn't making much money, but he was working. It wasn't going to be much of a Christmas, but he was providing for his family.

On Christmas Eve, everyone was at home. As the snow gently fell, a soft knock was heard at the front door. Benjamin went to answer it. There standing in the snow was the old clockmaker. Under his arm was a bundle wrapped in a big cloth. Excited, Benjamin invited him in. The clockmaker was his friend who had patiently answered all of his questions. Benjamin thought to himself that one day he wanted to be a clockmaker too.

Quietly, the old man entered the house. He took his cap off and greeted Benjamin's mom, dad, and sister. He handed the still-wrapped-up-clock to Benjamin. Not knowing what Benjamin had done, the family was certainly curious. "You should be very proud of your son; he is a fine boy . . . very bright and inquisitive!" Benjamin beamed and handed the clock to his dad. The clockmaker continued, "Your son wanted you to have this. It is his Christmas present to you."

Benjamin's dad gently unwrapped the clock. It gleamed as he removed the cloth. The clockmaker had fixed and timed it to perfection. He had polished the wood and made the enamel dial shine. It was transformed into a beautiful functioning clock. Benjamin's dad was stunned. The clock that he declared worthless just a few weeks before was now gleaming like it was brand new.

Benjamin was thrilled. The clockmaker grinned a broad grin that made him look even more like old Saint Nick. Benjamin's dad didn't know what to say. The old clockmaker broke the silence. "You have a mighty fine son who loves you very much. Benjamin brought me that old clock. He told me that he wanted it fixed just right so you would be proud of it and him. I have done my best." Benjamin beamed again.

The old clockmaker smiled and with a wink, silently left. Benjamin ran outside in the snow to thank and pay him. He hoped he had enough money. He wanted to thank and wish the old man a Merry Christmas. As he looked around, no one was in sight. No footprints in the snow. No sign of the old man at all.

Benjamin ran down the street to the old house where the old sign swung above the snow. He didn't understand. While he stood there, a lady passed by. "Are you looking for someone?" she asked. "Yes," he said. "I'm looking for the old clockmaker who lives in that house." The lady smiled. "Why, that old man? He died ten years ago. He was a good man, but he has been gone a long time."

Stunned, Benjamin slowly walked home. Silently he opened the door. He walked over to his dad's waiting arms. Softly his dad said, "Son, thank you for the best Christmas present ever. I love and am so proud of you!"

In the hands of the Master Clockmaker, all our lives can be changed. As we allow Him to fix our hurts and our shortcomings, He delights in shining us up and making us worthwhile in our own eyes again. Like Benjamin, his dad, and that old clock, sometimes we all get stuck. However you know Him let the Master Clockmaker do His work in your life. You will find yourself back in time and harmony with Him and with those around you, especially those whom you love most. Happy Holidays to all!

Amen and Amen

(This story will be released as an illustrated children's book in the fall of 2016. Watch for its availability on Amazon under the same title)

The Author

Phil has enjoyed watches and clocks since the mid-1990's when he bought his first "collectible" watches after checking out several time-related websites. He has loved writing ever since winning a poetry contest in fifth grade! Finally, all of you who know him know he loves a good story. *Reflections on Time* is a merger of these three loves. It is partly autobiographical as Phil shares the desires and struggles in his own life. The final story in the book "The Clock that Couldn't Tell Time" will be released in the fall 2016 as an illustrated children's book.

Phil retired twice, once from his position as deputy superintendent of business at San Diego Unified School District and once from his position as interim superintendent of the Sweetwater Union High School District. He also served as an associate professor of psychology and director of counseling, specializing in the integration of psychology and theology, and the teaching of homiletics. Phil also served as a licensed and ordained minister in the Mennonite and Baptist traditions.

Phil, Jeanne, and their son Chris now live full-time in the village where they enjoy watching the Palanganas River flow by their home. They grow pecans and assorted fruits and are beginning a small herd of Charolais cattle. Phil also continues to write. Last year he published an award-winning history of the impact of religion and the Mexican revolution on each other. His book has been adopted as a required text in Mexican religious studies. He is currently working on an analysis of the American public school district and a case study on doctrinal influences on religion as conflict, focusing on the 1857 Mountain Meadows Massacre in Utah. Please feel welcome to contact us via our website: http://www.riovistagroup.com.

www.ingramcontent.com/pod-product-compliance
Lightning Source LLC
Chambersburg PA
CBHW071542040426
42452CB00008B/1093